The Story of New Zealand's Unique Birds

Dedication

This book is dedicated to everyone anywhere who
would like to know more about New Zealand's
amazing birds that are found nowhere else on earth.

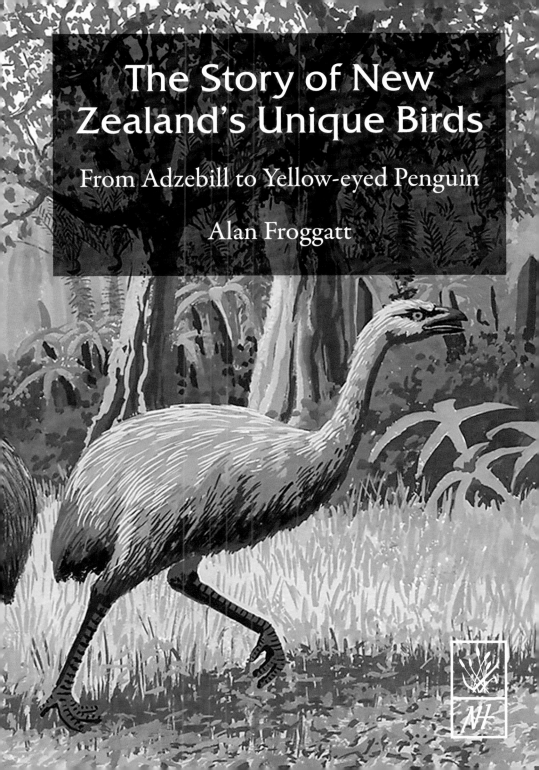

The Story of New Zealand's Unique Birds

From Adzebill to Yellow-eyed Penguin

Alan Froggatt

About the author

Alan Froggatt is a member of Birds New Zealand and
the Royal Forest and Bird Protection Society of New
Zealand; he was chair of the Kapiti Mana branch
of the society. He has extensive birding experience
throughout New Zealand and on a number of its
offshore islands, and has worked with the Nga Manu
Nature Reserve, the Pukorokoro Miranda Naturalists'
Trust and the Kapiti Environmental Restoration
and Maintenance Trust. Alan addresses schools and
public gatherings on birding and conservation issues.

Acknowledgements

I wish to thank the following individuals for their kind and various assistance in
helping me with this book: Andrew Digby, Kevin Hackwell, Jason Froggatt, Phil
Bilbrough, Brian Gill, Fiona Powell, Anita Totha, Emma Burns, Tatsiana Chypsanava,
David Riley, Matu Booth and Sarah Irvine.

The sources of any image not from the author's collection are acknowledged where
they appear. In this regard I wish to thank the following for their approval to use their
copyright and other images. Alan Tennyson, Craig Greer, Lindsay Froggatt, Kathy
Reid, Tony Whitehead, Glenda Rees and Andrew Digby.

I also wish to thank the following organisations for allowing me to use their
copyright and other images: Department of Conservation (DOC), Otago Museum,
Nelson Provincial Museum, Canterbury Museum, Kaikoura Museum, Museum of
New Plymouth Puke Ariki, Auckland War Memorial Museum Tamaki Paenga Hira,
National Library of New Zealand, Alexander Turnbull Library, National Museum
of New Zealand Te Papa Tongarewa, Land Information New Zealand (LINZ),
New Zealand Post, Isaac Conservation and Wildlife Trust, Radio New Zealand and
Allied Press.

I also need to thank the Public Library of Science Journals in San Francisco,
California, USA, for the image used on pages 2–3 (Creative Commons Attribution
cc-by 2.5 generic) (www.plos.org).

Lastly, I thank my wife Rosemary for her encouragement in helping me to
complete this project, and New Holland for their editing work, encouragement and
layout skills.

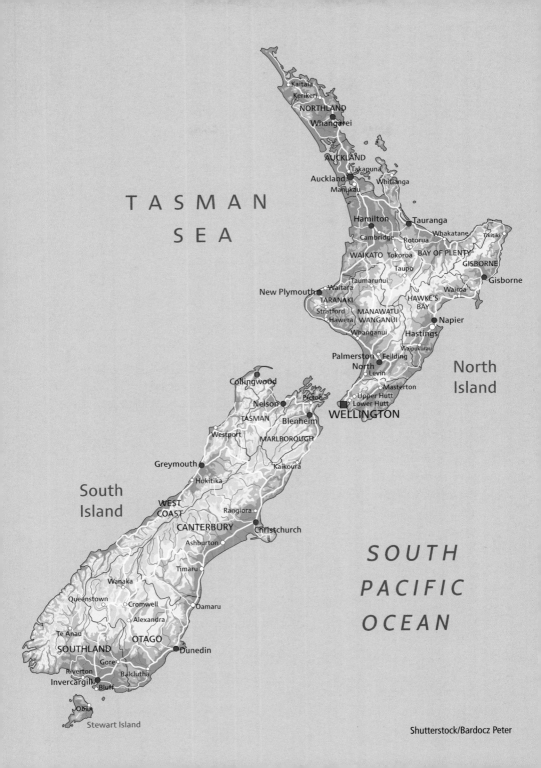

Contents

In The Beginning:
The Southern Avian Ark?

About 85 million years ago the islands that were to become New Zealand were born during periods of cataclysmic earthquakes and volcanic activity which broke up the southern supercontinent of Gondwana. Ten million years later the marginal chunky fragments that were to become New Zealand broke away from the Australian chunk and began their long drift out into the Pacific Ocean to their present location, which they reached after about 60 million years. Each chunk carried with it the flora and fauna it then possessed.

About 15 million years ago its mountains began rising. Further tectonic upheavals and volcanic activity helped shape its remarkable topography into the North and South Islands and many smaller islands of which the most significant in terms of contemporary bird life include Three Kings, Great Barrier, Poor Knights, Kawau, Chathams, Stewart, Ulva, Kapiti, Mana, D'Urville, Secretary and Tiritiri Matangi. Also included are the important Kermadec group in the north and the four Subantarctic island groups of the Bounty, Snares, Campbell and Antipodes lying across the westerly wind belt of the 'Roaring Forties'. The ancient geological processes also left 64 smaller offshore islands, numerous rock stacks, exposed reefs and volcanic cones, all of which fall within the geographical area of present-day New Zealand.

Today the main islands of New Zealand are approximately 1,600km in length and 400km wide at their maximum, with a coastline of 15,000km and a tendency towards mountain building, earthquakes and volcanic activity. It has a marked maritime climate and one that ranges from subtropical in the north to subantarctic in the south. On the South Island the east is divided from the west by the Southern Alps, while the west of the North Island is divided from the east in many areas by the Aorangi Range in the south, then in the north by the Tararua Range, Kaimanawa Range and Coromandel Range. The nearest neighbouring landmass is Australia, which lies 1,700km to the west across the Tasman Sea.

A natural science lab

Since New Zealand's geographical isolation, geological processes, in association with the impacts of weather events, produced a landmass with distinct types of habitat where many species of birds could live, feed and breed among mountains, swamps, lakes, rivers, estuaries, forests, open country, lakes and beaches. It also left a land where 90 per cent of the trees grew from seeds blown on the wind or carried by sea currents from Australia, New Guinea or South America. This created forests from the snowline to the waters' edge.

The islands hosted lifeforms with ancient Gondwanan lineages, such as podocarp forests and tuatara (a 200-million-year-old fossil has been found). There were no mammals except for bats and an extraordinarily diverse group of birds, of which the majority of species were endemic. Remarkably, the birds evolved to fill the ecological niches normally filled by mammals elsewhere on the planet. Fossil and subfossil records suggest that small mammals did once inhabit New Zealand, but these did not survive the rigours of the last few million years. As there was no longer any need to fly to escape from ground predators, many of New Zealand's birds became flightless or poor flyers.

New Zealand was the last major landmass in the world to be inhabited by humans, and was also the last primeval wilderness on the planet. Evidence of the avifauna that inhabited the islands prior to human arrival has been found in fossils and subfossils recovered from swamps, peat deposits, dunes and caves. Some of these have been dated as far back as 28.2 million years, but the most prolific deposits date back to around 30,000 years ago.

Over time many ancestral migrants to many of New Zealand's unique species were blown to the islands on the easterly winds from Australia, or floated or flew there from Australia, New Caledonia, Antarctica (which at the time was not covered by ice) or elsewhere.

Many evolved to become bigger, heavier and stranger than birds found anywhere else. All were descendants of birds that could fly but many lost the ability to do so. All they needed to do to escape aerial predators was hide on the ground or blend into the background. A detailed account of how all forms of life came to be on New Zealand and evolved can be found in Terry Thomsen's fascinating book, *The Lonely Islands: The evolutionary phenomenon that is New Zealand*.

As Charles Darwin explained in his famous book *On the Origin of Species*, speciation on islands took place leading to natural selection where variation occurred in species in the perpetual struggle to survive. This was to become known as the theory of vicariance. It is, however, much more complicated than this. Leon Croizat postulated his theory of dispersal, explaining that such variation and evolution occurred when a species was able to cross a barrier such as an ocean or mountain range. Then there is the theory of diversity. This explains that a single species can diversify into more species from a single hypothetical ancestor, as moa did. Indeed, recent research strongly contradicts continental vicariance and supports the theory of flighted dispersal. Modern molecular techniques can help provide confidence by resolving the Darwin-Croizat paradox and proving lineage on a case-by-case basis.

Whatever the case, the early avian arrivals have been in New Zealand long enough to evolve quite differently to their ancient ancestors. Some, like the moa, kiwi, weka and takahe, became flightless.

Many became different in shape. Some previously wetland species never set foot in water. Of our 250 or so native bird species, only about 100 are landbirds. By comparison, elsewhere in the world normally 90 per cent of bird species are landbirds. 85 per cent of these birds are endemic to New Zealand. That is, they occur nowhere else. In short, their ancestors in other countries are only very distantly related. In contrast, the British Isles, which is situated close to the main European landmass and was connected to it in the last ice age, has only one endemic species. Thus, it was that New Zealand became a biodiversity hot-spot.

Human arrivals

Some believe that the first humans arrived in New Zealand from the East Polynesian islands of Tahiti and Rarotonga in about AD 950, but no scientific evidence has ever been found to support this theory.

There is, however, evidence proving that separated groups began arriving from East Polynesia and settled in different parts of the country from about 1150 AD with most groups arriving in the North Island between around 1250 AD and 1300 AD to become collectively known as Te Ao Maori. Each group brought their individual beliefs, traditions and values with them and all were of warrior races. All these groups found a unique ecology and weird and wonderful birds that lived in forests, scrub and in the open. They brought with them the Kuri (Maori dog) and the agile voracious predator the Kiore (Pacific rat), and within 150 years had colonised the country.

They were quick to identify some of the larger flightless bird species as a ready food source, as they did the smaller native pigeon, kaka and other birds. They also used the feathers of some for their cloaks and ornamental purposes and left behind them middens (buried ovens and rubbish pits). These would often contain shells, fish bones, moa bones (moa is the generic word for chicken in Polynesia) and the bones of other birds they had eaten. One of these middens covered an area of 2.2 hectares and was by no means the largest.

When Captain James Cook arrived in New Zealand in 1769 on the *Endeavour* and found fur seals and whales aplenty, he unknowingly opened an environmental Pandora's box. While it was Abel Tasman who discovered and named the country in 1642, it was the accurate maps and navigation charts of Cook, the master navigator, that allowed the adventurous to seek their fortunes in New Zealand.

While Cook wrote in his journal of the wonders he had encountered it was the naturalist on the *Endeavour,* Joseph Banks, who alerted governments and society to the amazing birdlife when he wrote: 'The trees are filled from ground level to high in the canopy by glorious bird and insect life.' He continued: 'The morn I was awaked

Captain James Cook c.1779.
Painting by Sir Nathaniel Dance-Holland (1735–1811). © Te Papa

to the singing of birds ashore from whence we are distant not a quarter of a mile, the numbers of them were certainly very great who seemed to strain their throats with emulation perhaps... Their voices were certainly the most melodious wild musick I have ever heard, almost intimating small bells but with the most tuneable silver sound imaginable.'

When he visited Paihia on the North Island coast on the *Beagle* in 1835 Charles Darwin wrote: 'With regard to animals, it is a most remarkable fact, that so large an island, extending 700 miles in latitude, and in many parts ninety broad, with varied stations, a fine climate, and land of all heights, from 14,000 feet downwards, should not, except for one small rat, possess one indigenous animal.'

Large and voracious Norway rats were quick to escape from the *Endeavour* whenever the gangplank was lowered on shore, or a rope was passed ashore. Then ship rats soon found their way ashore from the vessels of the sealers and whalers. They too lost no time in feeding on ground-dwelling birds and their eggs and young.

Age of extinction

By the time the first flood of European settlers arrived in the 1840s, many species of bird were extinct. For the surviving species it only got worse. While it had taken Maori 800 years to destroy 50 per cent of the forests and 25 per cent of the grasslands, and they had initially farmed the Kiore as a food source, it only took 80 years for the European settlers to slash and burn another 25 per cent of forests as trees were felled for timber and land clearance for settlement and stock. By the 1850s several more bird species had been lost.

A.S. Thompson, an army surgeon who spent 11 years in New Zealand, wrote: 'It is high time good collections of the birds of New Zealand were made, as some have already disappeared, and the others are declining.'

The new waves of settlers brought cats as pets and dogs to work stock and pigs, indeed Captain Cook himself released pigs into New Zealand as a potential source of food. Unknown to the settlers they also brought mice as unexpected luggage. All of these mammals wrought devastation on birdlife.

Starting in 1869, and continuing for another 60 years, the European Hedgehog was introduced for sentimental reasons and to control slugs and snails in gardens. It too readily took the eggs of ground-nesting birds.

Brushtail possums were first introduced from Australia in 1837–40 and this process continued until the 1920s. This mammal eats forest leaves, twigs, flowers, berries and the fruit of many trees and shrubs. In the process it causes considerable damage to indigenous forests, exotic pine forests, farmland and orchards. It also carries bovine tuberculosis that can infect cattle. In 2019 Landcare Research estimated that possums ate 21,000 tonnes of vegetation each night. That's an annual total of 7,665,000 tonnes.

Later, when food for settlers was in short supply, rabbits were introduced to solve the problem. This may have appeared a satisfactory solution as these animals produce 4–12 kits four times a year, but rabbits being rabbits their numbers grew at a staggering rate.

An article entitled 'The Ornithology of New Zealand,' provided by an anonymous contributor and published in the scientific journal *Nature*, decried the extent of the acclimatisation 'mania' which was ousting native birds.

The discovery of gold in the North Island in 1842 and in the South Island in

Left to right: stoat (the apex predator), rat and possum. Courtesy of Radio New Zealand

1856 accelerated this process, altering for ever the former ecological system and thus bringing about a third wave of extinctions in New Zealand. In 1874 Walter Buller, the famed author of the ornithological classic *New Zealand Birds*, claimed in his second edition of 1838, that the country's native birds were doomed. In a way he himself helped this process for he shot many birds, collecting many species for overseas museums, private collections and conversation pieces for the Victorian wealthy.

The Land Act of 1892 allowed for the creation of scenic reserves and flora and fauna reserves and by 1901 these covered 607,501 hectares. This act recognized the fact that because of the long separation from any other large land areas, the flora and fauna that have evolved in New Zealand are vastly different from anything found elsewhere.

By the early 1900s things were so bad that the apex predator the stoat, and its mustelid cousins the ferret and weasel, were unwittingly introduced to kill the rabbits. Unfortunately, all of these predatrs soon realised that birds and their eggs and young were much easier prey. By now feral cats were also helping to decimate the birdlife.

While the causes of various species extinctions in the world are still debated, in New Zealand it is universally agreed that humans contributed to this by hunting, introducing mammalian predators, making changes to habitat through destruction by fire, clearance for timber, arable land, homes and roads, and in the search for gold.

14

Birdlife of New Zealand today

In 2019 New Zealand's remaining avifauna consisted of endemic, native and introduced birds. Endemic birds are those that only live and breed in New Zealand and are found nowhere else, for example the Tui. Endemic breeders only breed in New Zealand but can be found elsewhere outside the breeding season, for example the Long-tailed Cuckoo. Native species are those that existed in New Zealand prior to human arrival but may also be found breeding elsewhere, for example the Pukeko. Self-introduced species are recent arrivals that made their own way to New Zealand and established a population, such as the Silvereye. And introduced species are those deliberately brought to New Zealand by humans, for example the Australian Magpie. There are also migrant species that occur every year but spend part of the year elsewhere, and vagrant species which only occasionally make their way to New Zealand under their own steam.

Some scientists believe that some of the ancient migration of birds to New Zealand may have occurred via Antarctica as some coastal regions of the continent remained ice free until as recently as 30 million years ago.

Advances in DNA collection and analysis techniques have allowed scientists to better use taxonomy in deciding which bird belongs to which order, family, or subfamily. As explained above, a taxon is endemic if it is unique to a defined geographical area as a consequence of historical and ecological factors. Order-level of endemism means that all the species in an order of birds occur only in New Zealand, for example kiwi belongs to the endemic order Apterygiformes. However, DNA links have proven a link between kiwi and the extinct giant elephant birds from Madagascar.

In family-level endemics the family does not occur outside New Zealand. This indicates that the lineage has probably been in New Zealand over a long period. Non-endemic taxa such as New Zealand native species are likely to have arrived much more recently.

This book is about New Zealand's 'deep endemics', the remarkable and unique birds that can be found on the country's main islands. The ninth Edition of the *Concise Oxford English Dictionary* defines 'unique' as being 'unusual or remarkable,' and the birds that you will read about in the species accounts certainly fit this description.

Many of them have featured on the country's stamps, coins and bank notes, and in its marketing and tourism material. Many people around the world are familiar with the word kiwi, for it's the country's most famous bird and it is entrenched in the psyche of its people who are known and universally respected as 'kiwis'.

Please enjoy the stories of New Zealand's totally unique birds, from the time of early human arrival to the present, many of which can still be seen on either the North or South Islands, and some of which sadly now only exist in museums and collections.

The
Extinct

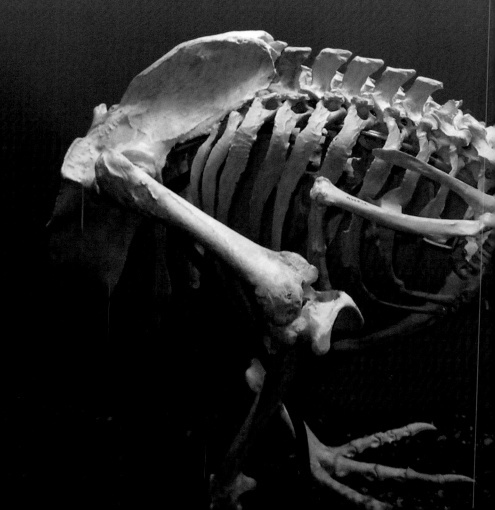

Adzebills

Order:	Gruiformes
Family:	Aptornithidae
Scientific names:	*Aptornis defossor* (South Island Adzebill),
	Aptornis otidiformis (North Island Adzebill)
New Zealand status:	Endemic
Conservation status:	Extinct c.1400

Adzebill stamp.
New Zealand Post

Some scientists regard these birds as New Zealand's most iconic animals. The adzebills were large, tank-like, flightless, terrestrial predators that were once widespread throughout both the North and South Islands, where they were restricted to dry open podocarp forests.

While they left behind no relatives to give clues to their behaviour, appearance or ecology, they were completely without wings, and had immense neck muscles, powerful legs and feet designed for vigorous scratching in the ground. They also had an enormous reinforced skull and a large pointed down-curving beak.

The adzebills weighed up to 19kg and measured nearly 1m in length. In terms of the evolutionary tree they were believed to have been a branch of the rail family. Their closest living relatives are the common pint-sized endemic flufftails from Africa, which are tiny skulking rails that are unlikely to be seen unless you are expressly looking for them.

A 19-million-year-old fossil discovered in the South Island suggest that the adzebills' ancestors flew to New Zealand. It is also thought the North Island Adzebill, which is 20 per cent smaller than its South Island counterpart, evolved after walking over the land bridge that once joined both islands.

Adzebills may have specialised in dismantling rotting logs in order to obtain invertebrates, and/or excavating burrowing animals such as tuatara or the chicks of nesting birds. While they were predominantly predators, isotope analysis has suggested that they may have also eaten berries, the leaves of soft herbaceous plants, small vertebrates such as lizards, and invertebrates such as spiders and insects.

An adzebill bone fashioned into an awl was found at the site of the Wairau Pa (Maori fortified village) in Marlborough. This and other evidence from middens (buried Maori cooking places and rubbish dumps) proves that they were hunted by early Maori and this may have been the cause of their extinction. Had they survived, they would have been among the world's largest birds.

Previous spread: **Skeleton of South Island Adzebill in Canterbury Museum.** Shutterstock/mikluha maklai

Bush Wren

Order:	Passeriformes
Family:	Acanthisittidae
Scientific name:	*Xenicus longipes*
Other names:	matuhituhi, matuhi, tom thumb bird
New Zealand status:	Endemic
Conservation status:	Extinct

Bush Wren. DOC

New Zealand wrens broke away from the passerine stock of Gondwana 58 million years ago during the Paleocene Epoch. Thus, they have the most ancient lineage of the country's endemic avian species. The family also included the Stout-legged Wren and the Long-billed Wren, both of which were extinct long before human arrival. All of these species are believed to have emerged after the Oligocene drowning of the country between 30 million and 25 million years ago.

There were three subspecies of Bush Wren, these being: North Island Bush Wren, *X.l. stokesii*; South Island Bush Wren, *X.l. longipes* and Stead's Bush Wren, *X.l. variabilis*, of Stewart Island and other offshore islands. All three are thought to have become extinct within 20 years of each other due to predation by rats and probably stoats.

In the 19th century Bush Wrens were usually seen alone or in pairs, sometimes several were seen together and the sprightliness of their movement and their silk-like plumage would catch the eye of observers. Maori believed that if you killed this bird snow would fall.

Any difference between the North and South Island populations was slight. North Island Bush Wren was originally recorded in the areas of Urewera, Lake Taupo, Remutaka Range and Days Bay near Wellington, but it was always local. Described by Walter Buller as abundant, it quickly became extremely rare.

South Island Bush Wren had been found in the high forested areas of Otago, the subalpine forests making up the inland boundary of Westland, in parts of Fiordland, and in many parts of the province of Nelson – particularly in the densely forested areas between Wallis Head and Tophouse and along the wooded banks of the Pelorus River in Marlborough. It was also seen in the Spencer Ranges of Marlborough at an elevation of 1,000m by a Mr Travers, the man after which the Travers Valley of Nelson Lakes National Park is named. The famed New Zealand geologist and explorer Sir James Douglas also encountered it, while the conservationist Richard Henry recorded seeing a number of these birds while employed from 1908 to 1911 as the ranger on Kapiti Island.

The population of Stead's Bush Wren appeared to be limited in 1931 to a number of the offshore islands of which Stewart Island was the most important. It was generally browner in plumage and had a less distinct eye-stripe.

As a small perching bird, the Bush Wren was seldom found on the ground. It had poor powers of flight and a weak but lively song. The sexes always called to each other using a subdued trill. At other times they used a faint rasp or loud *seep*, sometimes rapidly repeated, and a loud *cheep* when alarmed. They would run along the branches of trees with restless activity, peering into every crevice and searching the bark for invertebrates and their larvae to feed on.

The cup-shaped nest was located in a small hole or in the fork of a tree. The compact structure was composed entirely of green moss, oval in form with a small entrance on the side not far from the top, and so small as not to admit the tip of a little finger. When built in a fork this entrance was slightly hooded.

The last recorded Stewart Island sighting was in 1951, the final sighting of the North Island subspecies was from Lake Waikaremoana in 1955, and the last South Island Bush Wren was seen in 1968 at Moss Pass, Nelson Lakes National Park. A translocated population persisted on Kaimohu Island until 1972. This tiny bird vies with the South Island Kokako for having the unfortunate distinction of being the most recent New Zealand bird to become extinct. Its demise can probably be attributed to predation by Pacific Rats, Norway Rats, Ship Rats and Stoats.

Eyles's Harrier

Order:	Accipitriformes
Family:	Accipitridae
Scientific name:	*Circus teauteensis*
Other names:	pouakai, Forbes's harrier, giant harrier, New Zealand harrier
New Zealand status:	Endemic
Conservation status:	Extinct by around 1919

In 1840 Ernst Dieffenbach, the first trained scientist to work in New Zealand and a friend of Charles Darwin, spoke of evidence of a new kind of raptor. This top apex predator was eventually named after Jim Eyles, the former director of the Nelson and West Coast Museum. It is thought to have favoured North Island forests, with a particular liking for the Hawke's Bay area, but also inhabited other parts of both the North and South Islands where it preyed on kereru, kokako, kaka and smaller moa of up to 40kg.

At 60–70cm in height it was 20 to 30 per cent longer and four times the weight of the New Zealand native Swamp Harrier, while it also had a short shrill cry, a wingspan of 2m, longer legs, and was chunkier, heavier and stronger. It is thought that given its relatively short wings and stocky powerful feet it pursued its prey very aggressively. Evidence suggests there may have been two subspecies or species, with the North Island bird being much larger than the South Island one.

It is believed that Eyles's Harrier died out centuries ago, perhaps shortly after the arrival of the majority of waka (sea going canoes) from East Polynesia. Its demise is presumed to have resulted from habitat change, reductions in available prey, predation of eggs and chicks by Kiore and dogs, and consumption by Maori.

Intriguingly, when travelling in the Landsborough Valley on the West Coast in 1870, the explorer Charles Douglas shot and subsequently ate two raptors of notably large size. One possible explanation is that he chanced upon a remnant population of Eyles's Harrier. However, Maori people of the time insisted that this bird had not been seen in living memory.

The Australian Swamp Harrier, *Circus approximans*, did not become established in New Zealand until after the disappearance of the Eyles's Harrier. This suggests that as the birds were so similar the ecological systems of the country then could not then have supported both species.

In 2015 researchers from the University of Otago, Canterbury Museum and Te Papa examined the DNA of Eyles's Harrier and discovered that it was related to the much smaller Spotted Harrier, *Circus assimilis*, from Australia, with the two species diverging one to two million years ago. The habitat, food sources, and lack of competition from mammals in New Zealand enabled Eyles's Harrier to evolve into a larger and different species and become an example of giantism in birds.

In 1949 a complete skeleton of Eyles's Harrier was found in Pyramid Valley, North Canterbury; in 1955 it was presented to the Canterbury Museum where it can be seen today. The Natural History Museum in London, United Kingdom, is believed to have the only skin in existence.

Eyles's Harrier. Painting by Paul Martinson. © Te Papa

Finsch's Duck

Order:	Anseriformes
Family:	Anatidae
Scientific name:	*Chenonetta finschi*
New Zealand status:	Endemic
Conservation status:	Extinct between 15th and 17th centuries

The first bones of this species were found in 1870 by a boy in a cave at Earnscleugh in Central Otago. These were sent to Dr Otto Finsch in Germany, who passed them to Professor Van Beneden, who described the species and named it after Dr Finsch and then published his findings in 1875.

It was related to the Australian Wood Duck, but had a different morphology in terms of body size – it weighed up to 2kg – larger legs and relatively short wings, pointing to a terrestrial lifestyle.

Unlike most other ducks it favoured drier open areas rather than swamps, lakes or coastal regions.

It was once common and widespread throughout the eastern drylands of the North and South Islands, in places with annual rainfall less than 120cm. Like several other New Zealand species, it slowly lost the ability and capacity to engage in sustained flight. As it had readily available food sources and was not threatened by predators it had no need to do so.

Maori of the period claimed it made good eating and was a great delicacy.

The last record of a possible

Finsch's Duck. Painting by Paul Martinson. © Te Papa

sighting was in 1870 when a dog caught an unusual duck near Opotiki in the Bay of Plenty, which may have been a Finsch's Duck. However, it is thought more likely that the species became extinct between the late 15th and mid-17th centuries.

Haast's Eagle

Order:	Accipitriformes
Family:	Accipitridae
Scientific name:	*Hieraaetus moorei*
Other names:	pouaki, hokioi, *Aquila moorei, Harpagornis moorei*
New Zealand status:	Endemic
Conservation status:	Extinct c.1400s

In 1868 Julius von Haast, the first Director of the Canterbury Museum, sent his taxidermist Frederick Fuller to supervise the extraction of moa bones from the Glenmark swamp in North Canterbury. Frederick was not there long before he found large bones, but these looked more like those of a large bird of prey than a moa. When Haast received them, he declared them to be: 'a raptorial bird of enormous dimensions.' His 1871 description of this freakishly large raptor was subsequently published in the 1872 *Philosophical Institute of Canterbury Journal*.

Later, following the discovery of a complete skeleton of the eagle in a swamp at Castle Rock, Southland, the species was named *Harpagornis moorei* from the Greek *harpex*, meaning 'grappling hook.' This related to its formidable claws. This skeleton can be seen today in the Otago Museum.

In 2005 Michael Bounce and colleagues from Oxford University compared the mitochondrial DNA of two Haast's Eagle specimens with that of six living raptors. It came as a surprise to many when Haast's Eagle proved it be a distant cousin of the Australian Little Eagle, *Hieraaetus morphnoides*, which at just under 1kg is one of the smallest eagles in the world. Presumably Haast's Eagle's ancestors had arrived in New Zealand from New Guinea via Australia. Thus, the name *Harpagornis* has become as extinct as the bird it once described.

Haast's Eagle evolved in the unique ecological environment of prehistoric New Zealand and set a record-breaking example of island giantism because its new environment and ready food sources were so favourable.

Haast's Eagle skeletons have been found at 51 sites in the drier parts of the South Island, where the species ranged from sea level to the subalpine zone. However, it seems that few, if any, existed in the more forested North Island.

In 1940 Roger Duff, the then Curator of the Canterbury Museum, found a complete skull while looking for moa bones in Pyramid Valley swamp. He noted: 'Even the bare bones convey an impression of power and ferocity.'

The Haast's Eagle, was the largest and most magnificent bird of prey to have

Haast's Eagle. Painting by Paul Martinson. © Te Papa

Haast's Eagle, Pouakai skeleton, collected by Augustus Hamilton, Southland, 1892.
Otago Museum

ever existed and was the only bird in the world known as an apex predator of an ecosystem. Females were larger than males, weighing up to 17.8kg, with a body length up to 140cm and a wingspan up to 300cm. The thick talons measured up to 7cm long on the front toes and 11cm long on the hind toes – measurements which made them comparable with those of a Siberian Tiger's claws. Its massive vulture-like bill, measuring 130–150mm in length, could easily penetrate moa bones.

Feather remains found with skeletons were up to 9cm and sombre brown. Oral Maori history suggests that they were tinged with yellow and green, and that the bird had red feathers on its head.

Unlike plains and desert eagles it did not soar, glide or circle at high altitude. It was a forest and scrubland dweller which perched, watched, and waited in ambush. It had extraordinarily strong leg muscles ideal for perching and holding a victim. It also had

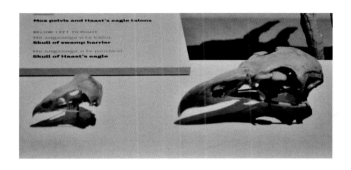

Swamp Harrier skull (left) and Haast's Eagle skull.   Haast's Eagle talons.

an amazing vertical leaping ability and exceptional eyesight. In short, it was a full-time contact predator and one of the most dangerous creatures that ever flew.

It fed on giant moa that weighed up to 250kg and measured 4m from bill to rump. It also ate ducks, weka, takahe, kakapo and other ground-living birds. Some scientists believe the kakapo evolved its unique camouflage to escape its attention.

For many years it was assumed that Haast's Eagle scavenged on the carcasses of moa trapped in swamps, or on carrion, but this theory changed in 1991 during another Pyramid Valley dig for moa bones when it was discovered 10 per cent of the Giant Moa bones recovered showed signs of the terrible impact of the eagle's high-speed strikes.

It attacked from the rear by diving at up to 80km per hour at the bird, clinging on its back and driving its talons full length into the kidneys, other vital organs and pelvis. It could also crush the bird's skull.

Despite its fearsome reputation the eagle's remains have been found in 50 midden sites in the South Island where some of the bones had been worked into tools. Centuries old Maori drawings of huge eagle-like birds were found in a cave in Craigmore in South Canterbury. In any event hunting this apex predator while wearing a seal skin or feather cloak must have put the hunter at a fair degree of risk.

Haast's Eagle lived for more than 2 million years before becoming extinct some 500–600 years ago. One study estimated there was a total population at 3,000–4,500 breeding pairs. Its extinction resulted from overhunting of its favourite food, the Giant Moa, by humans, together with loss of habitat and possibly direct hunting of the eagle by humans.

Two perfect skeletons were recently found in Honeycomb Hill Cave at Oparara on the West Coast of New Zealand. It is thought they had flown into the large dark green hole to feed on moa that had fallen in and could not get out. Another skeleton was found in a cave in Nelson. This one is held by Te Papa, where it now can be seen transformed into an impressive replica of what the bird looked like when alive.

Hodgen's Water-hen

Order:	Gruiformes
Family:	Rallidae
Scientific name:	*Tribonyx hodgenorum*
Other names:	New Zealand native-hen, *Gallinula hodgenorum*
New Zealand status:	Endemic
Conservation status:	Extinct

This small rail was related to the Black-tailed Native-hen and the Tasmanian Native-hen of Australia, but as an omnivorous, non-specialist feeder it was quite different. Its closest surviving relatives in New Zealand are the Pukeko and the South Island Takahe.

Hodgen's Water-hen occupied a range of habitats near forests in both the North and South Islands and appears to have been most abundant around the Hawke's Bay area of North Island. It was also widespread on the South Island where it favoured the more varied habitats.

Analysis of early Maori middens show that it was taken for food, while its eggs and chicks were probably taken by the Pacific Rat.

It was named after the Hodgen brothers who owned the Pyramid Valley Swamp where its fossil bones were found.

Hodgen's Water-hen. Painting by Paul Martinson. © Te Papa

Huia

Order:	Passeriformes
Family Name:	Callaeidae
Scientific Name:	*Heteralocha acutirostris*
Other name	New Zealand woodpecker
New Zealand status:	Endemic
Conservation status:	Extinct mid-1920s

Huia stamp.
New Zealand Post

Many ornithologists consider this large, spectacular, starling-like songbird to be a 'magical bird' and the greatest loss to the country's unique avifauna. It is thought to have evolved over millions of years from crow-like stock. Genetic comparison suggests it may share a common ancestor with the bowerbirds, berrypeckers and longbills of New Guinea. All of these are similar as they have rounded wings, limited powers of sustained flight

Mounted pair of Huia (female on left). © Te Papa

and use bounds, hops and jumps to move around the forest floor. When the first European settlers arrived it was the largest New Zealand songbird – at 300g it was 70g heavier than the next largest songbird, the North Island Kokako.

Maori considered the Huia tapu, or sacred, and thus protected it and it was only hunted in limited numbers. Its long bill and long black tail-feathers with white tips were highly prized for use as decoration, as marks of status, or as friendship tokens and for trade with other tribes. Its dried head and bill were also worn as ear ornaments.

A cache found in Central Otago in 1892 contained 70 tail feathers. These had been stored in a waka huia, an intricately carved wooden box similar to one presented by Maori to Captain Cook.

The early Maori of the area that today includes Wellington and Hawke's Bay hunted a certain group of Huia they called Huia-ariki, or chief of the huia. This bird was even rarer than the ordinary bird and was only presented to a chief of the very highest rank. It had a brownish instead of a greenish-black plumage, a banded grey tail, and alternating patterns of dark feathers on its neck and head. It is thought that this variation was probably due to a form of leucism.

Before 1769, as the result of the impact of Maori hunting, predation by Kiore and habitat loss, the Huia had disappeared from the northern half of the North Island. Yet in 1889 when the Earl of Onslow, the Governor General of New Zealand, asked an assembly of Maori chiefs what he should name his newborn son, they asked him to call the boy Huia, the name of their most sacred bird. One of the chiefs said: 'There yonder in the snow-clad Ruahine Ranges, the home of our favourite birds. We ask you, o Governor, to restrain the Pakaha (settlers) from shooting them, that when the boy grows up, he may see the beautiful bird that bears his name.'

This striking bird with large powerful legs and strong claws was the largest of the five New Zealand wattlebird species. In his book *Birds of New Zealand* Walter Buller wrote: 'In its flight it never leaves the shade of the forest and moves along the ground, or from tree to tree, with surprising alacrity, in a series of bounds or jumps (and never runs).' Other sources reported that the Huia was able to jump 20 feet (6m) at a time and would often bound with a slight opening of the wings.

Like all New Zealand wattlebirds, the Huia's wattles hung at the base of each side of the bill and were often held pressed under the chin. Males were 45cm long while females were 2cm longer. They weighed 300–400g. After its decline in the north of its range, the Huia was commonly found in the Remutaka, Tararua and Ruahine ranges and nearby forests of the lower North Island. The species has never been seen on the South Island.

This is the only bird in the world where bills of the the male and female were of a different shape and length. Typically, the male would use its bill as a pickaxe to dig into rotten wood, bark, lichen, moss or ferns on the ground for huhu larvae, weta, butterfly,

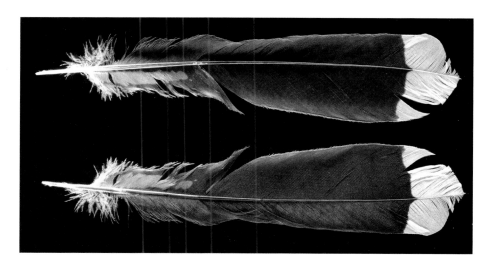

Huia tail-feathers. © Te Papa

caterpillars, spiders and other invertebrates, and it could also force its bill open to split the wood. It also ate native forest fruits including hinau, pigeonwood, coprosma, kahikatea and young leaves.

The male's hunting strategy often required the help of a female. While the male could tear away the outer part of a green sapling to get at the weta deep in its hole it required the female, with her much longer more curved and slender bill, to ensure success. Old-timers maintained the pairs hunted together. This appears to be confirmed by Walter Buller who wrote: 'Sometimes the male removed decayed wood to be able to peck out the grub, when the female would at once come to his aid and accomplish this with her long slender bill, which he failed to do.'

He went on to say: 'I noticed however that the female appropriated for her own use the morsel thus obtained. It's interesting to note while male to female transfer of food has been recorded the reverse has never been recorded.'

The male's most endearing actions were using its tail as a fan, showing the white tips to advantage, and caressing its mate with its ivory bill. Its soft tremulous flute-like melodious calls could be heard up to 400m away and Maori named the bird after its call. While they were often seen in pairs they would invariably respond quickly to a tremulous whistle or whimper and thus were easily shot.

Walter Buller wrote: 'They are hopping actively from branch to branch, and at short intervals balance themselves and spread out to their full extent their broad white-tipped tails, as in sheer delight; then the sexes meet for a moment to caress each other with their beautiful ivory bills, while they utter a low, whimpering love-note; and then, without any warning, as if moved by sudden inspiration, they bound off in company, flying and leaping in succession, to some favourite feeding place, far away in the depth of the forest.'

The Huia bred in monogamous pairs from September through to February with the male feeding the female during courting, nesting, and caring for the two to four eggs in an oddly-shaped oval nest. Pairs were recorded as being affectionate and excited, and when a female was captured the male easily allowed himself to be captured.

During the Duke of York's visit to New Zealand in 1902 a high-ranking Maori woman took a Huia feather from her hair and placed this in his hatband, thereby recognising him as a great chief. When this photograph appeared in the world press overseas museums and bird collectors rushed about buying whole stuffed specimens, but the Huia was known as a unique New Zealand bird long before this. These reports surrounding the duke's visit simply added urgency in the race to obtain specimens.

Entrepreneurs also lost little time in collecting specimens for sale as drawing-room conversation pieces. The Austrian naturalist Andreas Reischek took 212 pairs between 1877 and 1889. Walter Buller recorded that 11 Maori hunters took 646 skins from the forest between Manawatu Gorge and Akitio in one month in 1863. Thousands were exported overseas. The bills of many of these were used to make brooches and other ornaments. In 1890 the Government enacted protection measures making it illegal to kill the Huia, but these were largely ineffective. Two years later an edict was issued that no more Huia were to be killed.

When the Huia started becoming scarce Maori placed a rahui (restriction) on taking it until numbers recovered, but by then it had all but disappeared. Prior to the collapse some birds had been seen in poor condition, covered with ticks, and it is thought by some that a form of epidemic may have cotributed to its loss, although it is generally agreed that a combination of factors, of which habitat destruction and overhunting played the major roles, led to the Huia's extinction.

The last accepted sighting was made by Mr W. Smith in the company of three other persons on 28 December 1907 on Mount Holdsworth in the Southern Tararua Ranges near Wellington. The official view is that a few Huia may have persisted into the 1920s. An unconfirmed sighting was made on 28 December 1922 in York Bay on the Wellington coast. Interestingly Huia were seen in the same area of the Tararua Range on several occasions between 1840 and 1913, but the bird is now considered extinct – that is unless the capture of a live bird or compelling photographic evidence proves otherwise.

Images of the Huia have appeared on the New Zealand 1933 threepence stamp and on the 1942 and 1960 sixpence coins.

Laughing Owl

Order:	Strigiformes
Family:	Strigidae
Scientific name:	*Sceloglaux albifacies*
Other names:	whekau, *Ninox albifacies*
New Zealand status:	Endemic
Conservation status:	Extinct 1914

Laughing Owl, Otago Museum. © Alan Tennyson

The DNA of the Laughing Owl relates it to the wider family of hawk owls in the genus *Ninox*, and thus to the native New Zealand Morepork which is New Zealand's only remaining owl species. Although closely related to the Morepork, at up to 45cm in height, weighing around 600g and with a wingspan of around 50cm, it was twice as large and looked and behaved quite differently, resulting in it being placed in a separate genus. It also nested year after year in the same place.

Morepork.

Described in 1844 from a fossil specimen collected in Waikouaiti, near Dunedin, the Laughing Owl was strictly nocturnal and probably widely distributed on North, South and Stewart Islands. It had yellow eyes, a prominent bill, a small head and short stubby wings. While it could fly it was primarily a ground-feeder that preyed on a wide range of insects, small birds, lizards and mammals, and apparently favoured the Polynesian Kiore.

It frequented forest and open country but preferred to hunt on the forest floor. It would use its strong long legs to pounce on its prey, then carry it back to its roost where it would consume it whole. As with other owls, the indigestable parts such as bones would be regurgitated as pellets. Another favoured prey item was the tiny native New Zealand Owlet-nightjar, which was nocturnal and crepuscular but became extinct in the 13th century.

In 1875 Taylor White, a friend of Walter Buller, reported finding Laughing Owls nesting in a crevice in a limestone cliff two miles east of the Von River, in the Thompson Range overlooking Lake Wakatipu and Queenstown. He reported that the entrance to the nest was difficult to find and so narrow that the birds had to squeeze in to enter. He also noted that the male was very attentive to the female when the eggs are hatching during September and October. Interestingly, he observed the birds flying quite high and for a considerable distance, and also reported that they seemed to prefer flying on cold and drizzly nights when they would often laugh, and this sound would travel for a considerable distance.

This 'laughter' has been variously referred to as doleful shrieks to frequently repeated loud disquieting shrieks that would go on for some time. A Canterbury naturalist wrote: 'If its cry resembled laughter at all, it's the unintelligible outburst, the convulsive shouts of insanity.' One writer noted: 'It was not the sound one wanted to hear when alone in the bush at night.'

In the mid-1800s the Laughing Owl was widespread in Canterbury, but it then declined rapidly. Some sources suggest the demise of Kiore and this owl were related, and perhaps these were related to a combination of the arrival of ferrets and stoats, and forest clearance. Some believe that the owl's sudden demise may have resulted from an avian disease spread by an introduced species.

In 1909 a young Laughing Owl was photographed at its nest in a limestone fissure in South Canterbury. The last known specimen was found dead on a road at Blue Cliffs, Canterbury, in 1914. Despite the species then being considered extinct, credible reports of sightings and people hearing the owl's calls continued into the 1930s. A possible sighting near Opotiki in the 1940s was not verified. Like many other New Zealand species before it, the Laughing Owl had no real defences against the combined onslaughts of introduced predators such as stoats, ferrets, weasels and cats.

In 2019 a small group of scientists made their way to a site under the flanks of Mount Nicholas, overlooking lake Wakatipu, not far from Queenstown. Along the ridgeline they found a series of small crevices and rock shelters estimated to have been used continuously by Laughing Owls as nesting and roosting sites for more than 10,000 years. It was not until the remains found in this location were analysed that people realised how many species of New Zealand's small vertebrates and invertebrates had become extinct. For example, among other fauna identified, the bones of 43 species of birds were found, of which only four species survive today. Thus the discovery of this site provided an especially useful picture of the country's diverse and abundant small birdlife during prehistoric times.

Lyall's Wren

Order:	Passeriformes
Family:	Acanthisittidae
Scientific Name:	*Traversia lyalli*
Other names:	Stephens Island wren, Stephens Island rock wren, *Xenicus lyalli*
New Zealand status:	Endemic
Conservation status:	Extinct 1895

The order Passeriformes, more commonly known as perching birds, contains over half of the world's avian species. The Acanthisittidae family of New Zealand wrens are considered to represent a distinct and separate lineage within the passerines, with no other living relatives, although research efforts have been hindered by the Acanthisittidae family's notable attribute – a sad history of extinction.

There were six species of New Zealand wrens extant before humans arrived. Of these, four are extinct, and remarkably three of these were not identified until the 1980s. The four extinct species had no keel on the breastbone and therefore could not fly. Only five species of songbirds out of about 4,000 species were flightless, and all but one of these were species of New Zealand wrens.

The fourth of the flightless quartet was Lyall's Wren. At about 22g it is the smallest flightless bird known to have existed. This tiny, drab brown bird with a solid bill and big feet found temporary sanctuary from the Kiore on Stephens Island in Cook Strait. It was crepuscular, feeding at dusk, hiding among the rocks, and when disturbed ran quickly like a mouse. Subfossil bone discoveries indicate that it was once common on both the North and South Islands and was a relic of a family once widespread in New Zealand. They also suggest it was once a popular food source for Laughing Owls.

In 1882 lighthouse keeper David Lyall and a team of workers arrived on the island with their sheep and cattle to build and operate a lighthouse. One brought his cat, as did David Lyall. It was not long before Lyall's cat Tibbles delivered him an unusual-looking bird; and it continued doing so until proudly delivering the last of these in February 1894.

The same year A.W. Bethan, second engineer on the government schooner *Hinemoa*, gave some bird skins he had obtained from Lyall to assistant keeper, bird collector and dealer Henry Travers, who gave or sold one to Walter Buller. Buller subsequently wrote: 'There is probably nothing so refreshing to the soul of a naturalist as the discovery of a new species.' In 1895 he wrote to the *Transactions and Proceedings of the New Zealand Institute*: 'You will readily understand, therefore, how pleased I was at receiving ... the skin of a bird from Stephens Island which was entirely distinct from anything hitherto known.' He immediately recognised it as a new species, set about describing it, and sold it to Walter Rothschild for 50 pounds. At the time of Buller's death in 1906, Rothschild bragged that Buller only had one skin of a Lyall's Wren while he had nine and had paid a high price for them.

Lyall's Wren has sometimes infamously been reported as having been discovered and exterminated by a lighthouse keeper's cat. In reality the first two cats had rapidly multiplied and by 1899 the keepers were shooting them to keep numbers down. Major deforestation on the island also played a part in the demise of the wren.

Lyall's Wren. National Library of New Zealand.
Public Domain, Walter Lawry Buller (1838–1906)

The story does not end there. Previously, researchers have suggested that New Zealand was completely submerged for a period between 25 million and 21 million years ago, implying that all of New Zealand's unique plants and animals must have immigrated and diversified after that time. This theory is inconsistent, for instance, with what is known about the moa, where the different species all shared a common Gondwanan ancestor. A study by researchers at Adelaide University in Australia and Canterbury Museum into the country's Acanthisittidae wrens found the ancient divergencies among the wrens suggest they had been resident in New Zealand for more than 25 million years, and possibly as long as 50 million years, at which time New Zealand had become disconnected from the rest of Gondwana. They reported: 'As the wrens were largely poor fliers, or even flightless, some land must have remained above sea level throughout that period.' They also noted: 'This has important consequences for our understanding of the evolution of New Zealand's unique ecosystems.'

Recent phylogenic studies looking at improving knowledge of family trees for avian species have revealed novel relationships and have been able to suggest taxonomic revisions. This, coupled with the well-justified molecular clock analysis and an improved ability to recover genomic data from extinct organisms, may well provide further evidence against the hypothesis of a complete inundation of New Zealand during the Oligocene period between 33.9 million and 23 million years ago.

Moa

Studies of moa, which dominated the ecosystems of New Zealand, have been a source of many surprises, a major one being that they evolved on islands rather than on a continent, and that there were many species. Since these birds remain a hot subject for research there may well be more twists and turns in the future.

All species of moa became extinct before European arrival, so information about their ecological tolerances, population densities, mobility, breeding and feeding behaviour is scarce.

Moa were ratites, part of a diverse group of large birds of Gondwanan origin, which are unique in that they do not have a keel on the sternum and are therefore unable to fly. Other ratites include kiwi, ostriches, emus, cassowaries and rheas.

Recent DNA work has shown the moa shared a common ancestor with the South American tinamous, which are a sister group to the ratites. This implies that basal ratites did possess the ability to fly.

Moa were the world's most ungainly, awkward birds. Were it not for the giant elephant birds from Madagascar the giant moa would also have been the world's heaviest bird species. That the ancestors of moa survived the 'Oligocene Drowning' of 25–23 million years ago suggests that not all of New Zealand was submerged.

Since first being described in 1839 the taxonomy of a moa has remained contentious, with up to 64 different species and 20 genera assigned at different times. Matters have been complicated by the complex geological history of New Zealand, its significant regional variations in climate, variations in diet, sexual dimorphism within species, and above all the upheaval of the Southern Alps. At present, though, it is generally accepted there were nine species of moa contained within three family groups.

While each family group preferred a different habitat, ranging from high alpine tussock grassland to dense wet forest to swamps, each one adapted to cope so some overlap occurred. The smallest of these was the Little Bush Moa, which measured 50cm

Julius Ritter von Haast with collection of moa skeletons recovered from Glenmark, North Canterbury. Auckland Library, Sir George Grey Collection

Moa Family Tree

Dinornithidae

- South Island Giant Moa, *Dinornis robustus* – favoured forests at different altitudes. It is possible that all other species of moa evolved from this single Gondwanan survivor.

- North Island Giant Moa, *Dinornis novaezealandiae* – inhabited forests at different altitudes.

Megalapterygidae

- Upland Moa, *Megalapteryx didinus* – occurred in montane to subalpine habitats.

Emeidae

- Crested Moa, *Pachyornis australis* – preferred subalpine scrub and grasslands to those at high altitude.

- Heavy-footed Moa, *Pachyornis elephantopus* – was widely distributed except in tall wet forests and high-altitude scrublands.

- Mantell's Moa, *Pachyornis geranoides* – preferred dry inland scrublands and forests.

- Eastern Moa, *Emeus crassus* – inhabited the coastal areas and swamplands.

- Little Bush Moa, *Anomalopteryx didiformis* – favoured conifer and beech forests predominantly in Southland.

- Stout-legged Moa, *Euryapteryx curtus* – found in lowland open forest and coastal sites with a drier climate in North Island and in eastern regions of South Island.

and weighed 15kg. The Upland Moa had feathering on its lower legs rather than scaly skin, which helped to keep its feet warm and enabled it to walk on snow.

At up to 240cm in length and able to reach to heights of 360cm, the giant moa were the tallest birds ever to have walked on the planet. Females were larger than males and could weigh as much as 250kg. Like many large birds it had to swallow stones to grind up food in the gizzard. The average number of gizzard stones collected from *Dinornis robustus* was 220 greywake pebbles with a total weight of 2.75kg. The stomach of a 6,000-year-old *Dinornis robustus* recovered from the Pyramid Valley Swamp contained *Olearia* and *Coprosma* residue, the gizzard of this bird contained 500 stones each 5–60mm across with a combined weight of 5.6kg.

The booming call of *Dinornis* must have been heard from far off. While all moa were often depicted with necks extended, this was not typical behaviour. Like other ratites they bent their necks to feed on low-lying vegetation; ostrich and emu vertebrae

Giant moa stamp.
New Zealand Post

are held quite erect by comparison.

Giant moa were widespread across New Zealand, long lived, slow breeding but fast runners. Early Maori referred to them as a wind eater, for when running against the wind a bird would keep its mouth open. Primitive rock paintings suggest it may also have possessed a vicious kick.

This feathered monster snipped off and ate the twigs of plants such as daisy-bush, coprosma, veronia and olearia, and also favoured the berries and leaves of other species. They had a particular liking for young Lancewood or Horoeka trees, and amazingly these evolved to grow long sword-shaped and prickly leaves until the trunk was too tall for the moa to reach, at which time the leaves reverted to their former shape, size and structure.

Moa ranged over most of New Zealand and in winter migrated from the high country to the lowland forests and plains where food was more plentiful. Different sized and shaped moa occupied their own niches by feeding on different plant species, on different parts of the same plants, or on the same plants but in different seasons.

Early human arrivals in New Zealand were quick to recognise moa as a key source of food that could be captured with ease and lost no time in spearing and clubbing them to death. The generally preferred method of cooking was over koromiko wood, which gave the meat a better flavour than other wood. Centuries later, on discovering and investigating moa bones found in middens from this period, scientists decried this hunting as 'a profligate use of a key resource.'

William Williams, 1800–78. Explorer and Anglican Missionary. Lithograph made by Charles Baugniot, 1852. Alexander Turnbull Library

William Colenso, 1811–85. Naturalist, explorer and missionary. Seated self-portrait, 1868. Alexander Turnbull Library

The first indication to Europeans that giant birds lived in New Zealand came in 1838 when the missionaries William Colenso and William Williams were visiting the Rangitukia Pa at Waiopu in Poverty Bay and heard the name of a mystery bird. Later, during a visit to North Island's East Cape with Maori guides they found a huge footprint which their guide explained belonged to the monstrous bird called moa. At around the same time explorers, geologists and scientists stumbled upon similar stories.

It was not long before William Williams collected similar bones from the mud by various rivers on the East Coast and sent these by sea to Professor Richard Owen the British biologist, comparative anatomist and palaeontologist. Shortly after this eminent scientist opened the boxes he addressed the Zoological Society in London, and the word moa was soon recognised around the world.

In 1842 the missionary Richard Taylor explored a plain and found it littered with moa remains, assembling a collection that included 12 skulls and fragments of eggshell. He noted

Professor Richard Owen with moa skeleton. *Memoirs of the extinct wingless birds of New Zealand.* Vol 2. London: John Voorst, 1879, Plate XCVII. National Library of New Zealand

that the honeycomb structure of these bones indicated that they must have come from birds.

A year later he was visiting the mouth of the Waingongoro River with a Maori guide when in the sand before him he saw an unusually large bone. When his guide said: 'It's a moa bone,' he realised that the delta at the river mouth was covered with little mounds of these remains.

Gideon Algernon Mantell, 1790-1852. English surgeon, scientist and palaeontologist. Wood engraving, 1852. National Library of New Zealand

Soon similar discoveries were being made from the East Cape of the North Island to Southland and from coast to coast. As moa had an extremely low centre of gravity, many of the birds had been trapped in bogs and swamps or drowned in ponds, lakes, rivers or streams.

On 2 February 1848, the scientist Gideon Mantell declared before the Geographical Society in London: 'I think we may safely infer traces of the gigantic ostrich-like bird which have long since been obliterated from the world have been found in New Zealand.' This caused a worldwide sensation.

In 1852 his father, Thomas Mantell, undertook the first archaeological dig in New Zealand in a stream near Oamaru in North Otago and found a stone oven full of moa bones and eggs that had clearly been cooked and eaten by Maori, thus proving that moa and humans had shared the land.

Te Papa is in possession of a perforated complete moa egg measuring 240mm by 176mm (a plaster cast of this egg is held by Kaikoura Museum). This was found in 1857 in the open hands of a Maori hunter buried in the sitting position. This is the largest moa egg found to date – longer than any other by 27mm – and is presumed to have come from a giant moa. Only 36 whole moa eggs are known to be held in museums around the world.

As moa eggs vary greatly in size, a study is underway to try and determine which species laid which eggs, and this in turn should help provide a more accurate map of each species' habitat and movements. This work will look at shell thickness, size, the slit-shaped pores on the shell surface, and available DNA evidence. Through necessity much of this work will be undertaken using shell fragments.

Moa bones were found in swamps and caves, and exposed during the gold rush of the 1860s when almost every creek, stream and river and any other accessible parts of the country were exposed to the eye, pick, shovel or sluice of the miner. In all six of the nine moa species had major populations in Central Otago. While the Little Bush Moa, Crested Moa and North Island Giant Moa were apparently rare, the Heavy-footed Moa, Mantell's Moa and the Eastern Moa were hunted in large numbers by Maori according to evidence from 67 hunting sites.

Elsewhere large quantities of moa remains were also found in the Canterbury Plains, where food was abundant. Remains were also found in the Aorere Goldfields near Nelson, while a cave near Takaka Hill produced 2,000 remains. Moa remains found buried under 15m of sand in Central Otago in 1870 proved that the birds' feathers were up to 18cm long and reddish-brown with white tips.

During an 1872 excavation of Moa Bone Cave in Te Rae Kura (Redcliffs, near the city of Christchurch) archaeologists removed the evidence of years of European occupation and discovered Maori had occupied the site from the 14th century as a shelter and place of food preparation. They also unearthed many important finds, including a stone-lined oven containing layers of ashes and bones from six species of moa, stone tools and a moa bone with a cut made by a tool.

Since then repeated archaeological work has unearthed many more treasures. Many of these can be seen in the Canterbury Museum. In 1939, while working on his stepfather's farm near the mouth of the Wairau River in Marlborough, a 13-year-old Jim Eyles made the greatest archaeological discovery in New Zealand's history when he found a moa bone clearly cut by a tool and a stone adze nearby. Meanwhile his stepfather began digging up a lot of Maori tools while ploughing and it was

Plaster cast of a moa egg. Kaikoura Museum

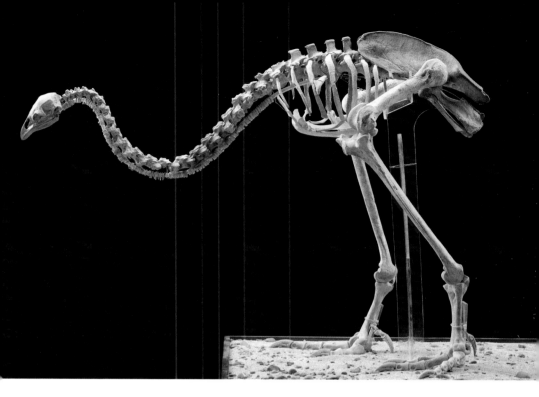

Upland Moa skeleton, collected by Josh Clark, Jonathan Carr and Trevor Worthy, Fiordland, 2003. Otago Museum Collection

not long before friends, neighbours and his father-in-law were fossicking in the area.

Late in 1939, with war looming, Jim was digging a defensive position on the farm beside the Wairau river estuary when he found a moa's egg measuring 20cm long by 14cm wide. Despite wartime restrictions fossicking continued to produce amazing adzes and other stone artefacts. Then in 1942, when digging beside a water tank near the house, he found a Maori grave full of priceless artefacts. Roger Duff, then ethnologist at the Canterbury Museum gathered a team and with Jim in attendance found a village containing hundreds of graves over a site thought to be up to 8 hectares. Nothing like it had been found before or since in the South Pacific. In time it produced a treasure trove of moa bones, eggs and an incredible range of stone tools and other priceless artefacts. It was this group of Maori that Duff referred to as moa hunters.

Usually extinction events can be seen in a species' genetic history – as numbers dwindle, they lose genetic diversity. But analysis of moa remains failed to find any evidence that the population was on the verge of collapse. On the contrary there is good evidence that the opposite was true. The birds' numbers were stable during the 400 years prior to their extinction. Further, they were robust, healthy populations when humans encountered and terminated them. It has been estimated that in the South Island alone half a million were killed and cooked.

Moa were hunted to extinction by Maori who ate their eggs, young and older birds, and lit fires to chase them out of the forest, burning important habitats in the process. All species of moa disappeared abruptly around 800 to 500 years ago. All that remained were their bones,

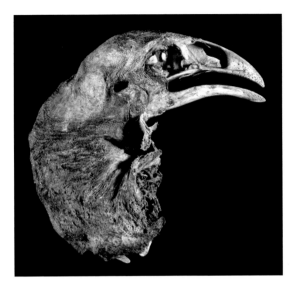

Mummified Upland Moa head found in Cromwell.
Te Papa

which were so abundant in places that settlers carried them away and ground them up for fertiliser. Research using carbon dating has found that the youngest bones tested dated no later than 1450 AD, thus supporting the hypotheses that moa were exterminated by the early human settlers in New Zealand.

Gone for ever were the great booming calls of the giant moa. Since they were the main food source for the Haast's Eagle it is no coincidence that this raptor disappeared at around the same time. For many years there has been an enduring belief that moa survived into the European era. This depended upon evidence that the Little Bush Moa may have survived in Fiordland until after 1770. The claims made of such sightings proved to be typical of those from other regions and parts of the world, combining patent mistakes and probable hoaxes. While some later reports demanded serious attention, thorough investigation found insufficient evidence to suggest that moa remained extant until this time.

The story does not stop here. Moa remain the subject of considerable research that will help to build a growing body of evidence in attempts to explore how other megafauna such as dinosaurs accommodate large bodies. In particular, the South Island Giant Moa (*Dinornis robustus* – translated as 'robust strange bird') attracts a lot of attention. A 2013 study using computer modelling looked at how it used its bones to move its big body. The results calculated that *D. robustus* was less heavy than previously thought, weighing roughly 200kg rather than 230kg.

This research suggests that as each species of moa evolved into its different form its bone mass changed according to its needs, i.e. *D. robustus* had a slower, more sluggish lifestyle than other species and therefore needed less bone density. This resulted in correspondingly lighter skeletal mass.

It is generally accepted that the rugged wilderness of Fiordland was the last home of the moa. Remains found in various places in Southland prove that these birds once inhabited this area from above the bush line to sea level in great numbers. The fact that there was no significant population of Maori in the cooler South Island until around some 500 years after their arrival in the North Island supports this hypothesis.

The skeleton of a moa was found near Queenstown in 1878 in a remarkably perfect state. The two legs and feet were complete with skin and feathers, the head was complete, skin unbroken and even the tongue preserved. It was initially thought that this bird may have been alive in 1820 or 1830 and may have been the last moa.

There was great excitement in May 2019 when a tractor driver found seven 70cm-wide fossilised moa footprints in the bed of the Kye Burn river on the Maniototo Plain of Otago – a remarkable discovery while he was exercising his boss's dog! Staff from the Otago Museum believe that these certainly date from before the last Ice Age 12,000 years ago and that they could possibly be millions of years old.

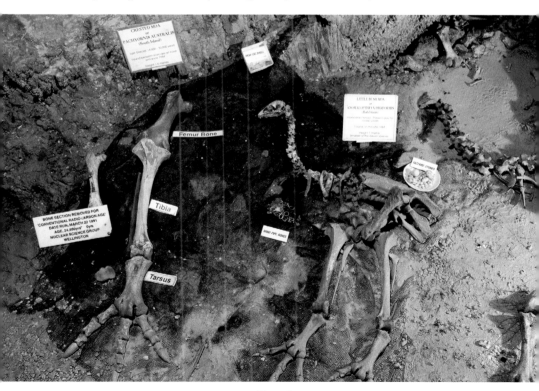

Moa dig.

New Zealand Little Bittern

Order:	Pelecaniformes
Family:	Ardeidae
Scientific Name:	*Ixobrychus novaezealandiae*
Other names:	brown bittern
New Zealand status:	Endemic
Conservation status:	Extinct

This bird was closely related to the widespread Australian Little Bittern and for years was regarded by many people as a race of that species, but this bird was larger, less stripy and had brown underparts. Hence it became known as the 'brown bittern' and was commonly found in the extensive swamplands extending from Waikanae to Rangitikei on the West Coast and in saltwater lagoons near the seashore. Fossil evidence from early Maori middens proved it was also found in Wellington.

It was shy, nocturnal and excelled at hiding itself. When emerging after the heat of the day, Walter Buller noted: 'It startles the ear with four booming notes – strongly repeated and representing the roar of an angry bull.' He also wrote: 'It is said to hate civilisation.'

The New Zealand Bittern was generally solitary and could stand for hours in one place. When seen it was usually either with its head bent forward watching the water for prey, or standing straight upright, almost perpendicular, in alarm posture. The stomach contents of a shot bird showed it ate mice, lizards, various species of freshwater fish and eels.

The species bred from September to January, normally producing four eggs on a flat platform of raupo. Eggs were incubated individually, with the result that the chicks were notably staggered in terms of size. Only the female incubated and fed them. The chicks had the habit of freezing like their parents. Adults were known to be aggressive when protecting their chicks and would stand erect, with neck and wings thrown forward, thrusting rapier like with the bill pointing at the intruder's face. It had a peculiar snapping cry.

Although never common, the New Zealand Little Bittern only became rare in about the 1880s. The last definitive record was in the 1890s. Its demise coincided with the arrival of the Kiore, Norway rat, ship rat, stoat, weasel and cat, all of which preyed on its eggs and chicks.

New Zealand Little Bittern. Painting by Paul Martinson, © Te Papa

New Zealand Coot

Order:	Gruiformes
Family:	Rallidae
Scientific name:	*Fulica prisca*
New Zealand status:	Endemic
Conservation status:	Extinct

This large bird, measuring 49cm and weighing 2kg, with a long neck and disproportionally long legs and toes, evolved from an ancestor similar to the Australian Coot. Its body proportions were similar to those of other coots and it was also probably capable of flight. However, unlike other coots it was more terrestrial and was found at forested inland sites as well as subalpine environments and coastal wetlands.

It probably formed part of the diet of the adzebills before becoming extinct around 200 years after human settlement, in all likelihood due to overhunting by Maori. Some of its bones found in two coastal middens in Marlborough had been fashioned into tools.

New Zealand Coot. Painting by Paul Martinson, © Te Papa

New Zealand geese

Order:	Anseriformes
Family:	Anatidae
Scientific name:	*Cnemiornis calcitrans* (South Island Goose)
	Cnemiornis gracilis (North Island Goose)
Other names:	North Island Goose, South Island Goose, tarepo
New Zealand status:	Endemic
Conservation status:	Extinct

The living relative of these two species is the locally introduced Cape Barren Goose, which is native to Australia. Of the two closely related New Zealand species the South Island Goose was the larger, measuring 100cm in length and weighing 18kg, making it comparable in size to a Little Moa.

Both New Zealand goose species were territorial, flightless, grazed on grass and had a modified toe which formed a spur which may have been used in fighting. The North Island bird was restricted to open county, forest margins, dune lands, grasslands, coastal margins and dry eastern areas, while the South Island bird preferred grasslands. Fossil records suggest that these birds were never common, and this was probably due to the limited extent of grasslands at the time. As an easy prey sprecies they became extinct soon after human arrival. Their bones were found in early Maori middens.

Cape Barren Goose is the extant close relative of
the two species of New Zealand geese.

New Zealand Owlet-nightjar

Order:	Aegotheliformes
Family:	Aegothelidae
Scientific name:	*Aegotheles novaezealandiae*
Other names:	St Bathans owlet-nightjar
New Zealand status:	Endemic
Conservation status:	Extinct

There are nine surviving species of owlet-nightjars worldwide. All of these shy birds occur in the region spanning from south-east Indonesia to Australia and New Caledonia, with the greatest species richness in New Guinea. These are small, short-billed, owl-like and mainly insectivorous.

At 150–200g the New Zealand Owlet-nightjar was three times the weight of the Australian species and a little larger than a Tui. It was the largest known species of owlet-nightjar and was closest to the endangered New Caledonian species which was also larger but had relatively small wings and large legs.

Like all owlet-nightjars it is presumed to have fed by catching prey such as frogs, geckos and other lizards at dusk and dawn. From the hundreds of fossil bones found it was determined to be probably a weak flyer or even unable to fly and most likely fed on the ground, although it was probably a good climber.

Because of its nocturnal and secretive habits it was rarely seen, but there are some interesting reports that it may have survived in New Zealand into the period of early European settlement. One report relates to a bird captured between tree roots on a creek bank in Canterbury in the 19th century which was 'exceedingly gentle' when handled. Another with mouse fur in its beak was knocked off a branch in the same region, while a third used a broken window to gain access to its daytime roost in a house.

Possible sightings on the West Coast include a 19th century report of a 'rare owl, smaller than a Morepork'. Fragmentary remains of an owlet-nightjar found in Haast Pass in the 1960s have unfortunately been lost.

New Zealand Owlet-nightjar was once widespread throughout New Zealand, where it frequented forested areas and dense scrubland and nested in dark holes. It had a particular liking for caves and a possible nest site was found in the entrance to a cave on Takaka Hill near Nelson.

As no confirmed evidence of its remains have been found in early Maori middens it is thought that the species may have quickly fallen victim to the Kiore.

New Zealand Owlet-nightjar. Painting Paul Martinson, © Te Papa

New Zealand Quail

Order:	Galliformes
Family:	Phasianidae
Scientific name:	*Coturnix novaezelandiae*
Other name:	koreke
New Zealand status:	Endemic
Conservation status:	Extinct

A naturalist on Cook's first voyage to New Zealand in 1769–70 may have been the first European to see this plump 200g bird, but it was not formally named until 1830 following a specimen that was collected on the North Shore of Auckland.

Once considered a subspecies of the Australian Stubble Quail, the New Zealand Quail belonged to the same genus but was larger and had different plumage. Like the Stubble Quail it was recorded as flying in small flocks or coveys and engaging in dust baths.

In the early 19th century it was commonly found across the country, favouring scrub and open grassland, and apparently it was more abundant on South Island. It was extensively hunted by the early European settlers for food and recreation. In 1848 Sir David Munro and Major Richardson shot 56 in one day in Nelson. At that time is was also abundant in Marlborough and Canterbury, although less common on the plains around Taupo. For the next decade a bag of 20 was considered a good day's shooting. One hunter recorded shooting more than 60 before breakfast on the spot where Cathedral Square in Christchurch now stands.

As a result of sports shooting, in association with the burning of its lowland tussock habitat to create grassland for stock, the New Zealand Quail abruptly declined and was seldom seen after 1865. The last known South Island specimens were taken either in 1867 or 1868 and the last North Island sighting was in Taranaki in 1869.

It came as a surprise to sport shooters and naturalists alike when it was declared extinct in 1875. Many claim it most likely fell victim to cats and Norway rats.

New Zealand Quail. Painting by Edward Lodge, UK, © Te Papa

New Zealand Raven

Order:	Passeriformes
Family:	Corvidae
Scientific Name:	*Corvus antipodum*; North Island subspecies *C.a. antipodum*; South Island subspecies *C.a. pycrafti*
New Zealand status:	Endemic
Conservation status:	Extinct

Weighing up to 1kg, the New Zealand Raven was one of the largest of the world's 5,000 or so songbird species, with only the likes of the Common Raven of the Northern Hemisphere, the Thick-billed Raven of Ethiopia and the Superb Lyrebird of Australia being heavier.

Most ravens and crows are similar in body shape, plumage and behaviour, so the likelihood is that the New Zealand bird was glossy black, had relatively long legs, a broad pointed bill and retained strong powers of flight.

It was once common around coastal New Zealand and was probably a raucous inhabitant of sealion and seal colonies where it would have eaten unprotected pups, eggs and offal. It probably also fed on fish, snails, shellfish and skinks. The presence of raven bones in the middens of early Maori show that they ate it.

It most likely died out as a consequence of the rapid elimination of the seal colonies for pelts by early sealers combined with overhunting for food.

New Zealand Raven. Painting by Paul Martinson, © Te Papa

North Island Snipe

Order:	Charadriiformes
Family:	Scolopacidae
Scientific name:	*Coenocorypha barrierensis*
Other names:	Little Barrier snipe
New Zealand status:	Endemic
Conservation status:	Extinct

This richly patterned bird with a 4cm-long bill and short legs, wings and tail is one of six species in the genus *Coenocorypha*, and was the only species of snipe found on the New Zealand mainland.

A specimen collected on Little Barrier Island, off the east coast of the northern North Island, by Captain Bennett of the schooner *Mary Ann* in about 1870 was acquired by the Auckland Museum. The only records of possible sightings prior to 1870 were on Motukorea Island in the inner Hauraki Gulf in 1820.

The bones of North Island Snipe have been found in sand dune deposits in Northland, cave deposits in the King Country and in Hawke's Bay and the Wairarapa. They have also been found in a lake-bed deposit in Hawke's Bay. It is thought that the species may have inhabited forested areas and was probably wiped out by the Pacific Rat.

North Island Snipe. Painting by Paul Martinson, © Te Papa

North Island Takahe

Order:	Gruiformes
Family:	Rallidae
Scientific name:	*Porphyrio mantelli*
Other name:	moho
New Zealand status:	Endemic
Conservation status:	Extinct

Walter Baldock Durrant Mantell, 1820-95.
National Library of New Zealand

In 1847 Walter Baldock Durrant Mantell, settler, adventurer and son of Gideon Algernon Mantell, was looking for moa remains with Maori guides in the Waingongoro River in Taranaki when he noticed some strange-looking bones. His guides promptly identified these as being from a takahe or moho. This species was subsequently named *Notornis mantelli* in his honour but considered to be extinct. It was often known by the Maori name of Moho.

It was the heaviest and largest rail species in the world. Fossil records show it favoured podocarp hardwood forests, swamps and dunes, but was able to successfully occupy a range of habitats from lowland forests to high-altitude valleys.

Like the South Island Takahe it had lost the ability to fly. At 4.1kg it was larger than the South Island bird and had longer legs. It had been lost from most of its original habitat before European arrival – as with the moa, Maori hunted it as a source of food.

Intriguingly, recent evidence suggests that the North Island and South Island Takahe evolved independently following the separate arrivals of Pukeko-like ancestors in New Zealand.

There is tantalizing evidence to suggest that the species may have survived until at least the late 1800s, with reports of a bird caught in the Ruahine Ranges in the 1890s causing wild excitement.

North Island Takahe.
Painting by Paul Martinson, © Te Papa

Piopio

Order:	Passeriformes
Family:	Oriolidae
Scientific names:	*Turnagra tanagra* (North Island Piopio)
	Turnagra capensis (South Island Piopio)
Other names:	North Island thrush, native thrush, New Zealand thrush,
	piopio-kate, korohe, tintiu, pipii, kata (laughing tiutu)
New Zealand status:	Endemic
Conservation status:	Extinct

Measuring 26cm and weighing 130g, these were large birds with distinctive strongly developed bills. They were creatures of the forest floor. Both closely related piopio species are now extinct, with the North Island Piopio declared extinct in 1947.

Piopio stamp. New Zealand Post

A recent DNA study revealed that piopio were related to the Old World orioles, a group of songbirds that are typically bright yellow and black elsewhere, but more sombre olive and brown in Australasia. As the oriole group originated about 20 million years ago, the ancestral species of the piopio must have arrived by dispersal across the Tasman.

Subfossil evidence suggests that the North Island Piopio, while uncommon, occurred from the far north of the island to Gisborne and the Wairarapa, up to at least 900m above sea level in matai broadleaf forests near Hawke's Bay and in the Urewera forests near Lake Waikaremoana.

One observer reported: 'It searches among the bush, snaps at the fruit stalks of moss, picking the seeds of trailing veronica. Its progress in general is usually delicate, it hops along with both feet together, a stiff fluttering of the wings and a flit of the tail accompanying each motion. When approached too closely to its perch it always descends to a site near to or on the ground.'

Both piopio species inhabited dense undergrowth, rarely flew, and had a tame and confiding nature. They were inquisitive, agile, nimble, and fed on insects, worms, berries, fruit, seeds and foliage. They would often stand on one leg, raking the surface with the other seeking worms and insects. While little evidence of the breeding behaviour is known, they nested in a fork of a tree in dense foliage and lined the nest with soft tree fern.

The South Island bird could be found in forests in the Lake Hauroko region of Southland, in Dunedin, and in the far north region of Nelson. Evidence of the South Island Piopio has been found in Canterbury's limestone landscapes. It would often

Piopio. New Plymouth Library, Puke Ariki

visit the huts and tents of bushmen and goldminers looking for food. Occasionally it would enter huts and tents in its search. During a trip to the West Coast Sir James Hector reported counting 40 by his camp. The birds would regularly investigate people camping, where they were easily killed by dogs, and were so common that it seemed inconceivable that the species would be extinct within 100 years. But by 1894 piopio were in fast decline on both the North and South Islands. Some birds may have taken refuge on Stephens Island, but this has yet to be confirmed.

Due to the resemblance of the South Island bird to the smaller Song Thrush introduced by the European settlers, they knew it as the native thrush. It gave a whistling series of five distinct bars which it repeated six or seven times in succession, rather like the Song Thrush. Maori thought that this sounded like ominous laughter, so the piopio became recognised by them as a bird that brought bad luck. It could, however, mimic the sounds of other birds.

The piopio was, in Buller's opinion: 'The best of New Zealand's songbirds,' but Charles Douglas disagreed. He wrote: 'It has no song, and its cry is a harsh twitter, a note the bird is evidently ashamed of and seldom uses.'

The last South Island Piopio sightings were at Lake Hauroko and Caswell Sound in Fiordland in 1947. The last known North Island Piopio was shot at Ohura in February 1907. There was an unconfirmed sighting in 1970 when an adult and two chicks were observed in the Hauhungaroa Ranges, in what is now Pureora Forest Park. There is evidence to suggest that settlers may have eaten piopio, and stoats certainly did.

Scarlett's Duck

Order:	Anseriformes
Family:	Anatidae
Scientific name:	*Malacorhynchus scarletti*
Other names:	New Zealand pink-eared duck
New Zealand status:	Endemic
Conservation status:	Extinct

Australian Pink-eared Duck is a close relative of the extinct Scarlett's Duck. © Craig Greer

Scarlett's Duck was widely but sparsely distributed in swamp lands and on shallow lakes in North Otago, the Canterbury Plains, Hawke's Bay and the Chatham Islands.

Its Australian cousin, the Pink-eared Duck, is the only other member of the genus *Malacorhynchus*, and has occurred in New Zealand as a vagrant. At 800g Scarlett's Duck was twice as large, probably similar in appearance, and fully flighted and aquatic. As a specialised filter feeder it fed on small organisms on the surface, including microcrustaceans such as ostracods and cladocerans. It probably preferred the open water of wetlands and lagoons and did not dive for food.

As a desired food source, Scarlett's Duck became extinct shortly after early human arrival and its nests were probably predated by Kiore.

South Island Kokako

Order:	Passeriformes
Family:	Callaeidae
Scientific name:	*Callaeas cinerea*
Other names:	orange-wattled crow, kaka, cinereous wattlebird
New Zealand status:	Endemic
Conservation status:	Considered extinct

The probably extinct South Island Kokako and the still extant North Island Kokako belong to the New Zealand wattlebird family Callaeidae, which also includes the extinct Huia and endangered North Island and South Island Saddlebacks. The only discernible difference between the two kokako species was the South Island bird had yellow or orange wattles rather than the blue of the North Island species.

Molecular studies support the theory that the ancestors of kokako arrived in New Zealand via Australia between 39 million and 34 million years ago. In doing so they may have island-hopped across the Tasman Sea using the now-submerged islands of the Lord Howe Rise and Norfolk Ridge as well as the prevailing westerly wind.

A total of 18 South Island Kokako were shot during Captain Cook's time in Dusky Sound in Fiordland and Queen Charlotte Sound in Marlborough.

Given that the kokako can produce long and beautifully clear notes, some have described it as the organ bird or flute bird. Others have said it has a woodwind voice. One of New Zealand's earliest conservationists, Thomas Henry Potts, described the male's very sweet six-note whistle as *te, to, ta, tu, tu, tu* and observed that the female sings one note less than the male. The song had a lower pitch than those of other birds, helping the sound to broadcast through the dense forest.

In February 1863 Charlie Henry Douglas was exploring and surveying the Matukituki Valley at the south-east end of Lake Wanaka when he saw and drew a picture of a South Island Kokako. He wrote: 'Their notes are very few, but the sweetest and most mellow tones I ever heard a bird produce.'

The male would display before a chosen female, arching its neck, spreading its wings and dancing in what Walter Buller described as: 'A very ludicrous manner.' He also reported that a Maori told him he had seen 20 South Island Kokako traveling rapidly over the ground with rapid hops and in single file.

Nests tended to be loosely constructed from leaves and twigs, but always have a well-fashioned cup, and located in dense foliage. One large oval nest found in Fiordland measured 30cm. In good seasons a clutch would consist of two or three eggs.

For many years the South Island Kokako, with its orange wattles and longer

Charles Henry Douglas and A.P. Harper taking a break by the Cook River, West Coast.
John Debree Pascoe Collection. Alexander Turnbull Library

legs, was considered extinct. That was until one was seen in Mt Aspiring National Park in 1967. The last confirmed sighting was near Reefton on the West Coast in 2007. This record was officially accepted as genuine by the Ornithological Society of New Zealand in 2013. The society has rated another 11 sightings during the period 1990–2008 as possible or probable.

In 2013 the New Zealand DOC changed the conservation status of the South Island Kokako, which is also known as the 'grey ghost,' from extinct to data deficient, pending any information that it can authenticate, and it continues to encourage interested parties to put evidence forward.

Then, in 2016, the DOC announced that it would support recovery efforts if proof of a living South Island Kokako is found. In response, in 2017 the South Island Kokako Charitable Trust announced a reward of $5,000 for confirmation that the bird still survives. This was later doubled to $10,000 by the promise of a donation from the Morgan Foundation.

Today a few stalwarts believe that the South Island Kokako survives in a secluded place in the Nelson Lakes National Park, but so far all their efforts to find hard evidence have failed. Therefore it seems highly likely that this species is extinct.

South Island Kokako was almost identical to its close relative the North Island Kokako (pictured) except that the former had orange-yellow wattles rather than blue.
Shutterstock/William Booth

The
Survivors

Bellbird

Order:	Passeriformes
Family:	Meliphagidae
Scientific name:	*Anthornis melanura*
Other names	korimako, makomako, mockie, bell bird, New Zealand bellbird
New Zealand status:	Endemic
Conservation status:	Not threatened

The nectar-eating Bellbird has an undulating and very rapid flight, a maximum life span of eight years and was the cornerstone of the famous dawn choruses of the forests which were much enjoyed by the early settlers. It is still a pleasure today for those lucky enough to hear it.

This species is the sole surviving member of its genus. The three living subspecies are the nominate form, which occurs on the New Zealand mainland and is considered 'Not threatened', and two island subspecies – Three Kings Bellbird, *A.m. obscura*, and Poor Knights Bellbird, *A.m. oneho* – both of which are listed as 'At risk.' The only other member of this endemic genus was the extinct Chatham Bellbird, *A. melanocephala*.

When the Bellbird sings it arches out its back and puffs out its chest. The song can be mistaken for that of the Tui, but is much more mellifluous. In general it has three

Bellbird.

different songs but these can vary enormously from place to place, and in 1859 one enthralled observer wrote: 'The lovely notes of the bellbird woke the sleeper with its sweet ringing chimes. Where there are a great number the leader gave the signal to begin singing with a sharp snap of its beak, and all the surrounding bellbirds joined in the chime, keeping perfect time together, till the leader, with another snap, gave the permit for a rest.'

Bellbird feeding on pollen in flax flowers.
Shutterstock/Southernlight

In the ship's log during his first visit to Dusky Sound in 1773, Captain Cook wrote: 'The ship lay at a distance from the shore; in the morning we were rewarded by the singing of birds, the number was incredible, and the singers seemed to strain their throats to emulate each other. This melody was far superior to any we have heard in the same land, it sounded like small bells finely tuned.'

Bellbirds were clearly very common prior to the arrival of Europeans, but a sudden decline occurred around 1860 which has been blamed on rats and disease. However, the species has persisted well compared to many of New Zealand's endemic birds and it is still relatively common and widespread today.

These attractive songsters prefer to nest in the same locality each year. They usually have two clutches annually and will lay these in a concave nest made of small twigs and lined with a deep layer of feathers. Bellbirds can be found in forest remnants, gardens, exotic plantations, forests and orchards. Outside the nesting season they will travel long distances seeking the flowers of native and exotic trees and shrubs, using their brush-like tongues to reach deeply into flowers seeking nectar. Because they also feed on the fruits that result from this pollination, Bellbirds play an important role in seed dispersal and assisting in forest regeneration.

Black-billed Gull

Order:	Charadriiformes
Family:	Laridae
Scientific name:	*Larus bulleri*
Other names:	tarapuka, Buller's gull, seagull, *Chroicocephalus bulleri*
New Zealand status:	Endemic
Conservation status:	Nationally Critical

Black-billed Gull is the world's most threatened gull species. Compared to the commoner Red-billed and Southern Black-backed Gulls it is less likely to be seen in towns and cities, and less commonly seen scavenging for food from human sources.

The species breeds on sparsely vegetated gravel islands on inland riverbeds, coastal shell banks, sandbanks and, when driven out by flooding, on farmland. World Wildlife Management International has reported an overall population decline of 78 per cent in 30 years, although the species appears to be expanding its breeding range along the North Island coastline with small numbers now breeding as far north as Kaipara Harbour.

The Black-billed Gull seldom nests in isolated pairs, preferring to breed in colonies which can sometimes incorporate thousands of nests. These are established in August or September with the breeding season running from December through to February. Most pairs will lay two eggs but clutches of four or more have been observed. A successful nest usually requires an island site surrounded by water to protect against predators. It also needs little or no vegetation for good all-round visibility, a good supply of food

Black-billed Gull.

close at hand, and little or no disturbance. It's not unusual to find nests abandoned due to flooding, predation or disturbance caused by human behaviour. Disturbing protected birds and destroying nests in New Zealand is an offence under the Wildlife Act 1953 and can result in imprisonment and/or a fine of up to $100,000.

During the breeding season this gull prefers to feed on invertebrates taken from rivers and adjacent pasture. It continues to use agricultural land in winter but will also feed on fish and marine invertebrates in the coastal marine zone.

A recent national aerial photography count of nests on the braided rivers through to single-channel rivers and streams of the South Island identified 60,256 Black-billed Gull nests. Of these 55.9 per cent were in Southland, 4.6 per cent in Otago, 34.3 per cent in Canterbury, 0.6 per cent in Marlborough, 0.3 per cent in Tasman and 2.6 per cent in the West Coast.

In January 2019, the Hawke's Bay Regional Council reported the good news that a colony of 600 pairs was nesting in Haumoana Road Bay, not far from the city of Napier.

Uncharacteristically, in July 2019 about 300 Black-billed Gulls established a breeding colony of 130 nests in the part-demolished and flooded foundations of a former office block in Armagh Street, Christchurch, which was protected by security fencing. This unusual event succeeded in attracting considerable attention from ornithologists, scientists, the DOC and the interested public.

Black-billed Gulls nesting in the central business district in Christchurch City.
Lindsay Froggatt

Black-fronted Tern

Order:	Charadriiformes
Family:	Sternidae
Scientific name:	*Chlidonias albostriatus*
Other names:	tarapiroe, sea martin, plough bird
New Zealand status:	Endemic
Conservation status:	Nationally endangered

This handsome bird with a vigorous swooping flight and staccato call has a range that is primarily based on South Island. It once bred in at least one site on the North Island volcanic plateau, but today it is a non-breeding visitor to the Cook Strait coast of North Island.

Measuring 290mm and weighing 95g, it mainly feeds on rivers, lakes and deltas in the south, but it will often follow farmers as they plough, picking up worms and grubs from the newly turned earth. It's for this reason that early settlers knew it as the 'plough bird.' As it also feeds on skinks, caterpillars, grass grub larvae and other farm pests, the Black-fronted Tern is welcomed by agriculturalists.

It moves rapidly in flight, often quickly changing direction as it catches quarry such as moths, small beetles and other insects on the wing. During the breeding period it feeds on hatching mayfly nymphs, stoneflies and small fish by contact dipping. Feeding activity is often accompanied by a lot of calling.

As a colonial breeder the Black-fronted Tern favours the distinctive wildlife and plant communities found in the braided riverbeds such as the upper Waitaki Basin and some other riverbeds and lakes in the South Island, occurring well up into the mountain areas. In these places it nests in colonies ranging in size from two to 50 pairs on open shingle, laying eggs on the bare ground. This preference gives the parents the best chance of spotting approaching predators, and vigorously and loudly defending their nest. Groups of adults work together to avert danger by dive-bombing any potential threat, while uttering their repetitive *kit-kit* calls. They often attack in a zigzag fashion, uttering harsh cries and aiming at the intruder's head, often only swerving away at the last moment.

Some Black-fronted Tern colonies are struggling. Those on the Upper Clarence and Acheron Rivers in Molesworth Station, Marlborough, had very low breeding success rates in the early 2010s, fledging only an average of 0.18, 0.08 and 0.10 chicks per nest over a period of three years. Following these results, nest sites were improved through the clearance of weeds, so that predators could not hide, and through enlarging the river channels around the breeding islands to make it more difficult for predators to reach the nests. Also, 281 predators were caught in the network around

Black-fronted Tern.

the three protected sites, including hedgehogs, stoats, ferrets, weasels and wild cats. As a result, in the 2016–17 breeding season nesting productivity was five times higher at these sites compared to colonies without protection.

In 2018 steps were put in place to assess what adaptations or further measures might be needed with sites selected for monitoring up until 2020. This work was carried out by Wildlife Management International Ltd and jointly funded by Environment Canterbury Braided River Regional Initiative, the Kaikoura Water Zone Committee's Immediate Steps Funding and the DOC. In the future it is hoped that this work will be continued by members of the community as part of their contribution to New Zealand's goal of being Predator Free by 2050.

Even with reduced numbers of predators, breeding on a riverbed is a risky business. Due to floods many eggs and chicks do not survive. As a mechanism to ensure the survival of its species, Black-fronted Terns can lay a second clutch if eggs or chicks are lost.

After breeding the birds disperse widely to coastal areas or sheltered bays, estuaries and lagoons, and this partial migration sometimes sees flocks numbering 200–300 birds. Some cross the Cook Strait and venture as far north as Kaipara Harbour, and these non-breeding birds will feed up to 50km from shore, taking mostly planktonic crustaceans.

Black Stilt

Order:	Charadriiformes
Family:	Recurvirostridae
Scientific name:	*Himantopus novaezelandiae*
Other names:	kaki
New Zealand status:	Endemic
Conservation status:	Nationally Critical

Black Stilt stamp.
New Zealand Post

This bird is regarded by Maori as a taonga, or living treasure. Prior to European colonisation it was widespread and abundant throughout the country, but it is now among the handful of rarest birds in the world.

In the 19th century this often solitary, sharp eyed, tough and versatile little wader with a long thin bill and extremely long thin legs nested over much of the South Island and as far north as Rotorua in the North Island. Most early accounts by settlers describe it as occurring from Hawke's Bay in the North Island to Southland in the South Island.

In 1888 Walter Buller stated: 'It is generally found in all the river courses of the Wellington district and further south.' By 1890 it had disappeared as a breeding bird from the North Island, and from Nelson, Marlborough and Westland in the South Island, and was declining in the remaining areas of the eastern South Island. Between 1910 and 1915 numbers declined in the North Canterbury rivers.

In 1918 an ambitious programme began to address the complex issues associated with managing the Black Stilt in the wild. Between the 1940s and early 1960s it only nested on riverbeds and swamps in South Canterbury and Otago, where it had become non migratory, and the total population had crashed to just 100 birds.

Black Stilts could also be found in associated small mountain tarns, rivers and lake edges, and on the river deltas and braided channels of the Cass, Ahuriri, Hopkins and Godley river valleys, but by 1970 it had disappeared from both the Hopkins and Godley.

In 1981, with only eight pairs of Black Stilts remaining, the DOC took on the responsibility of saving the species from certain extinction by implementing an intensive captive-breeding programme based on obtaining clutches of eggs from the wild, artificially incubating these in special breeding facilities at Twizel in Canterbury, and rearing the chicks to three or four weeks old before returning them to the wild.

Several wild birds are held for breeding purposes under the captive-breeding programme. Their eggs are artificially incubated, and the young chicks are raised in captivity. These programmes are conducted in tandem with intensive predator control and public information and educational programmes. In 2017 there were still only

132 birds living in the wild. Of the 120 chicks returned annually to the wild, only 33 per cent survive to adulthood.

Since recovering from the low-point of eight pairs in the 1980s, the Black Stilt population has favoured the Tasman River valley in the tough Mackenzie Basin in the Southern Alps in central South Island. This area seems to hold a fascination for many people in New Zealand. It is a land of legend, a land of contrasts, of vast open spaces, endless flats, famous mountains, cloudless skies, heat and bitter cold, a land noted for its rivers and wonderful lakes, yet also renowned for droughts.

Black Stilt.

Known as a place for hardy pioneer settlements, it is still a hard land from which to make a living. Some claim that the weather there can match either Antarctica or the Sahara, and conditions are certainly unpredictable, with temperatures dropping to −30°C and climbing in excess of 40°C. Despite the tough conditions in their last outpost, Black Stilts can survive for up to 12 years in the wild.

Since 1977 work on the Black Stilt has been supported by the Isaac Conservation Trust, which in 2009 was changed to the Issac Conservation and Wildlife Trust, with processes put in place to ensure that its objectives will continue to be met into the future.

In recent years a few Black Stilts have been seen far from the Mackenzie Basin, in the Ashley River estuary near the city of Christchurch, and there have been unconfirmed sightings on the West Coast.

The Black Stilt is relatively solitary compared to the similar-looking Pied Stilt, which is more inclined to form groups with others of its own kind. It has a larger body, longer wings, a more robust bill and shorter legs. These birds use their strong and versatile bills to feed by snatching, plunging, pecking, scything, probing and raking for small fish, molluscs and larvae of various aquatic insects.

Normally monogamous, the Black Stilt will breed when aged two or three years. One problem is hybridisation – with such a small population, in cases where a Black Stilt cannot find another of its kind as a mate, it will pair up with a Pied Stilt and produce hybrid offspring.

Both male and female Black Stilts will aggressively defend the nest whilst giving high-pitched yapping alarm calls. Another strategy, shared with other species of shorebirds, is to feign a broken wing in order to lure predators away from the eggs or young. The camouflaged patterning of both the eggs and chicks make them very difficult to locate, but even so they are easy prey for feral cats, rats, stoats and ferrets.

Brown Creeper

Order:	Passeriformes
Family:	Pachycephalidae
Scientific Name:	*Mohoua novaeseelandiae*
Other Names:	New Zealand brown creeper, New Zealand titmouse, pipipi
New Zealand status:	Endemic
Conservation status:	Common within range

This noisy little songbird favours a range of habitats from sea level to the tree line on South and Stewart Islands. It likes beech and podocarp forests, manuka and kanuka scrub and regenerating forests, and can also be found in willow, gorse, broom, exotic pine forests and some grasslands.

When feeding it will often move about in small family groups, foraging acrobatically about 2m off the ground for beetles, moths, spiders and caterpillars, and will sometimes hang upside-down to do so. It's not unusual for the flocks to associate with other species such as Tomtit, Silvereye and Yellowhead.

The Brown Creeper is non-migratory and has a sweet melodious voice and a range of chattering contact calls and trills, including a single *chip* and a *cheer* call. While both sexes sing, the male's song is louder and more complex with sequences of 5–14 notes. While groups normally feed silently, one bird may break into song and inspire the entire flock to sing in concert. The male weighs 13.5g and the female 11g. While some may have a life expectancy of more than 10 years, the average lifespan is thought to be about five years.

Brown Creepers show high levels of fidelity with 64.7 per cent of pairs lasting more than two seasons and 29.4 per cent lasting three seasons. Losses are more the result of death by disease rather than divorce or mate swapping. The birds defend their territory all year with nesting beginning in September and finishing in late November after successive clutches. During the first period of nesting and laying the male will closely guard the female and defend their breeding territory with bouts of loud and prolonged singing. Sometimes the female will join in to chase intruders away. Nests are placed in dense cover in the tree canopy and sometimes in shrubs or low trees 1–10m above the ground. A clutch of 2–4 eggs are laid, 63 per cent of the eggs will hatch and 36 per cent will fledge to produce an average of 1.6 fledglings per successful nest. Birds can breed at 12 months of age.

This species and the Yellowhead are the only South Island birds that are hosts to both the brood-parasitic Long-tailed Cuckoo and Shining Bronze-Cuckoo. The female cuckoo will remove a single egg from the host nest and replace this with one of her own. The Brown Creeper seems to accept this, and a pair will feed the much larger

Brown Creeper. © Glenda Rees

cuckoo chick. After hatching and before gaining its sight, the cuckoo chick will eject other eggs and any nestlings from the nest by pushing them out with its feet.

The creeper helps to cope with this predation by laying its first clutch before the cuckoos make their annual return to New Zealand.

Brown Teal

Order:	Anseriformes
Family:	Anatidae
Scientific name:	*Anas chlorotis*
Other names:	brown duck, pateke
New Zealand status:	Endemic
Conservation status:	Recovering

Brown Teal (male on left).

This elegant, small, primarily nocturnal dabbling duck is rather timid and skulking, but it is fiercely territorial and prefers habitats with heavy vegetation where it can hide during the day. It was once common in lowland swamps, swamp forests and brackish slow-flowing rivers throughout the country. As it evolved it became more terrestrial in its habits than is typical of most ducks.

Since the 1990s, when it was considered effectively extinct in the South Island, it has been confined to the North Island where a total population of about 1,000 birds exists in Northland and the Coromandel. A few others can be found in wildlife sanctuaries on both islands that are authorised by the DOC to breed them for release into the wild.

The male has a piping trill call while the female has a growl or uses a high-pitched rapid *quack*. On emerging at sunset, Brown Teal will swim downstream to a place of rendezvous, then fly in flocks to feeding grounds, often around lakes, where they will

Brown Teal with ducklings.

remain alert all night making peculiar musical notes as they feed on the shoots of water plants and invertebrates. Occasionally they may dabble in shallow water to filter out small food items such as fish. If disturbed they will normally swim away rather than fly.

When visiting a settlers' bush camp in Eketahuna in the Wairarapa, and writing of the 'brown duck,' Walter Buller wrote: 'I found them after dark in a drain happily feeding alongside the road. They were very tame, allowing me to approach within a few feet of them.'

On another occasion he noted: 'I came upon a flock of 60 or more of the birds. Instead of taking wing they closely followed each other to the shore, then forming into line hurried forward in a most impetuous manner, keeping close under the bank of the lake, while uttering a low confused twitter.'

The successful recovery of this New Zealand icon is the direct result of DOC activities supported by Ngatiawa Iwi, who want to see the birds return to their ancestral tribal lands. It is also supported by those breeding the birds for release at considerable personal cost. The Isaac Conservation and Wildlife Trust provide facilities for pre-release conditioning and processing, that is banding, transmitter attachment, disease screening and so on. Community groups also help by carrying out intensive predator control at sites with good habitat.

Meanwhile DOC is working hard to establish populations in Abel Tasman National Park in Nelson and in Fiordland National Park. Despite all these efforts this bird remains the rarest waterfowl species on the mainland.

Blue Duck

Order:	Anseriformes
Family:	Anatidae
Scientific Name:	*Hymenolaimus malachorhynchos*
Other names:	whio, mountain duck, blue mountain duck
New Zealand status:	Endemic
Conservation status:	Nationally Vulnerable

Blue Duck stamp.
New Zealand Post

The image of this slate-grey torrent-loving duck with a chestnut-flecked breast appears on the country's ten-dollar bank notes and on a 1987 issue of its 40-cent stamp. It's seldom seen far from fast-flowing mountain streams where it can dive and swim with ease as its body is streamlined to allow the water to flow over it.

Although it appears to be a strong flier, the Blue Duck seldom does so; if it flies at all it will do so low over the surface of the water directly to another stretch of river. The male has a distinctive *whio-whio-whio* whistle, from which the Maori name whio is derived. The female's call is a vibrating or clattering *cra-ack*.

Prior to human arrival its range extended from high altitude tarns, lakes, and rivers to segments of bush lowlands, rivers, and lakes. Until recently it was exceedingly rare but now may be found in a few clear fast-flowing turbulent rivers with a gradient of 50–80m fall per kilometre and streams in the Bay of Plenty and those flowing from the central volcanic region of the North Island. It can also be found in the high mountain regions of Fiordland where waterways provide the ideal habitat of stable river channel, coarse riverbed substrata, narrow stream width, riparian edges and the water runs clear and clean.

Blue Ducks are monogamous and fiercely territorial, and bond pairs are maintained throughout the year. Once established the territory is generally held for life. On average one pair need one kilometre of river to feed and breed, and they will attack any other Blue Ducks and kill their ducklings if they encroach on the territory. However, when food is plentiful Blue Ducks have been known to allow another pair to share their territory.

The diet is almost exclusively made up of freshwater invertebrates, of which caddisfly larvae form a key constituent. As trout also feed heavily on these larvae, the number of trout residing in a river can have an adverse impact on this food source. The soft protuberance on the end of its bill allows the Blue Duck to scrape larvae and insects from the surface of rocks, while the well-developed claws on its feet allow it to easily climb boulders and hang onto these under water. Berries from streamside plants have been recorded in the diet of Blue Ducks living in alpine areas, but not elsewhere.

Blue Duck.

Blue Duck nests are well hidden close to the favoured stream, in locations such as hollow logs, holes in the riverbank, at the base of fern clumps, beneath fallen trees or in dense vegetation. This makes the nesting female particularly vulnerable to attack by stoats and possums, while rats and weka have been implicated in nest and egg destruction. While the female incubates the eggs for 33–35 days the male will wait in attendance nearby.

The chicks are guarded by both parents until fledging at 70–80 days and the brood is raised entirely within the territory. When the adults begin their post-breeding cycle and have completed moulting, they will evict the offspring from the territory, but not from the same river catchment.

Adult Blue Ducks are adept at protecting their chicks by feigning difficulty to entice the enemy into pursuit. The ducklings take to the water within a few days of hatching, can easily dive and are expert swimmers.

Despite the DOC implementing a ten-year plan in 2009 to protect existing populations and resettle and protect other pairs in suitable environments, the Blue Duck remains under threat from predators, burgeoning tourism and habitat loss due to the growing demands for water sources for hydroelectric power generation and irrigation.

Young Blue Ducks with adult on the right.

Efforts have been made to release birds into suitable habitat and 2020 was a stellar year in this respect. Following the release of 63 birds in Taranaki in March 2019, 87 ducklings were found in a total of eight rivers in Taranaki and on Mount Taranaki. With 31 known breeding pairs, the Taranaki birds have taken a significant step in establishing a self-sustaining population. This has only become possible as a result of enhanced predator control on the mountain by volunteers and by farmers owning nearby land. Other releases include eight birds in the Arthur Valley in Fiordland, the home of the famous Milford Track.

As the Blue Duck is only found on clean and clear streams it is recognised as an indicator species for water quality. There would be few bushmen or deer hunters for whom the *whio whio* whistle of this duck would not bring back a nostalgic longing to return to the heart of the bush, high up in the forest, with the mountain tops glimpsed through the canopy, a rushing torrent cascading over large boulders and rocks, here and there a still pool, the home of Blue Duck and perhaps a trout or two.

Fernbird

Order:	Passeriformes
Family:	Megaluridae
Scientific name:	*Bowdleria punctata*; North Island subspecies *vealeae*; South Island subspecies *punctata*
Other names:	koroatito, karoti, matata, u-tick, New Zealand Fernbird
New Zealand status:	Endemic
Conservation status:	Declining
Other information:	Other subspecies can be found on Stewart Island, Whenua Hou and the Snares Islands.

This wary, well-camouflaged, curious, skulking bird is about the size of a sparrow and is fond of swamps, wetlands and scrub, where it creeps about furtively like a mouse. It is unique among birds in that its tail-feathers are disconnected. As it can scuttle through dense undergrowth at a good pace its tail-feathers are usually frayed and worn. With short wings and a ragged sparse tail, it is reluctant to fly in the open; when it does fly it rarely travels more than 30–40m.

Fernbird.

In Walter Buller's day it was widespread in bracken and low scrub, but this changed when settlers began draining the land and burning off the scrub. However, it is still found today in residual swamps, in scrubby types of coastal saltmarsh among sedges and oioi (jointed rush), and in poor fern and scrubland.

When seen it is unlikely to be confused with any other New Zealand species. The North and South Island subspecies differ only slightly in terms of plumage. The Fernbird is more often heard than seen, and is best identified by its high-pitched cry of *u-tick, u-tick* or *oo-tik*. Curious to see what is happening when two small stone are clicked together, it will often poke its head out for a look, then quickly display before returning to cover.

Fernbird nest. Image taken by John Charles McLean, 1818-1902.
Auckland War Memorial Museum, Tamaki Paenga Hira

Buller wrote: 'In the Manawatu district there is a continuous raupo swamp, containing an area of 50,000 acres. Save for the piercing cry of pukeko, occasionally heard, and the boom of the lonely bittern, the only sound I could detect was the cry of this little bird calling to its fellows in this tangled mass of reeds.'

Typically 3–5 eggs are produced in October–November in a small cup-shaped nest less than 1m above the ground. This is constructed from dry grass, sedges and leaves, then lined with feathers, and will often have a hood as protection from the wind and rain. Both parents incubate the eggs, which take about 14 days to hatch, and care for the chicks until they fledge at around 16 days. Up to three clutches may be produced in a season. At maturity Fernbirds weigh about 35g and can measure 18cm.

This species is potentially an important indicator of wetland health as it is dependent on the presence of high-quality diverse habitats and rich food supplies. Today it can be found in locations such as: Tongariro National Park among tussock, flax and bracken; the King Country; Kahurangi National Park near Nelson; Catlins on the Otago coast, and in some areas of the West Coast. Thanks to successful translocations from Lake Rotokare Ecosanctuary in Taranaki, Fernbirds can now be found in the Pauatahanui Wildlife Reserve just north of Wellington and the nearby Mana Island sanctuary.

Fiordland Crested Penguin

Order:	Sphenisciformes
Family:	Spheniscidae
Scientific name:	*Eudyptes pachyrhynchus*
Other Names:	tawaki, New Zealand crested penguin, thick-billed penguin, Victoria penguin, Fiordland penguin
New Zealand status:	Endemic
Conservation status:	Nationally Vulnerable

This bird is one of the rarest penguins in the world and the only crested penguin to inhabit the main islands and coast of New Zealand. The first specimen was collected by Robert McCormick, the surgeon and scientist on the HMS *Erebus* and HMS *Terror* Expedition of the early 1840s, and donated to the British Museum.

Subfossil records suggest that the Fiordland Crested Penguin was once more widespread, ranging up to the southern parts of North Island, and that it was probably common in parts of the northern South Island.

Along with the Emperor Penguin of Antarctica it is the only penguin species to breed in winter. It nests mainly in Fiordland in late winter, in loose muddy colonies a short distance inland, usually in dense forest which is hard to access. It favours headlands, inlets and areas around the entrances to fiords. More recently its nests, which are the most substantial nests of any penguin, have been found in a few other coastal areas. Two of these sites are located in Milford Sound which the famous British author and world traveller Rudyard Kipling claimed to be: 'The eighth wonder of the world.' Given that 700cm of rain falls there every year it is mostly very wet!

Breeding begins in loose colonies in July and continues through to November, with nests positioned 1–3m apart. These are typically located under fallen trees, roots or boulders, or in rock crevices, caves or underground warrens. Two eggs are laid over 3–6 days with the second being larger than the first. Typically only one chick is raised, but in favourable years two chicks have been raised successfully in up to 12 per cent of breeding pairs.

Eggs are laid on the feet, then enveloped inside the brood patch in late July and August. The chicks are fed by both parents at intervals of 1–3 days, with one parent guarding the chick or chicks for the first two weeks or so before the new chicks are left in an unattended colony while the parents go to sea, travelling distances of up to 15km and diving to depths of up to 160m in search of food.

At this point the chicks typically form into small creches, which they leave after about 75 days. They are fed by both parents until fully fledged, at which time they go

Fiordland Crested Penguin. Shutterstock/John Yunker

to sea. Their calls include loud braying or trumpeting, high-pitched contact calls and low-pitched hissing and growling.

Some have been seen returning to their nest-sites to moult from mid-January to early March. This is an incredibly stressful time because unlike other avian species penguins moult catastrophically by losing all their worn feathers before replacing these with new ones. During this period, which normally lasts around three weeks, each bird will lose around half its body weight, be unable to swim, and is at the risk of starvation, dehydration and increased dangers from predator and human disturbance.

The greatest threat to eggs and chicks is from introduced predators, while the greatest threat to adults is from a significant reduction in the populations of squid which typically make up 80 per cent of the diet, while set and inshore trawl nets have an estimated bycatch rate of 176 birds per year. Oil spills pose an extreme risk to the nesting birds. A dramatic rise in tourism numbers has resulted in increasing disturbance around nest sites which these birds can find intolerable.

Since 2014 the Tawaki Project at Jackson Head on the West Coast has been studying the foraging behaviour, reproductive success, population developments and breeding range of these birds. Miniature GPS satellite-tracking devices and dive loggers have been fitted to 20 selected birds to track their movements in real time, studying their habits on land and at sea before and after breeding. Researchers were surprised to find that the birds travelled as far as the Auckland Islands, Macquarie Island and halfway to Antarctica within a couple of weeks. The champion of the group swam almost 7,000km in two months. In the words of one scientist: 'It was insane.'

Researchers think that the journeys into Subantarctic waters may be instinctual, but are unsure as to why the birds are willing to expend so much energy doing so and suspect that it may be for a key food source. Other research shows a complex pattern across the brains of all waterbirds. As the brains of their ancestors enlarged and developed to modify the flight stroke for diving, so the brain of this penguin appears to have enlarged slowly. It's believed this may be linked to sensory modifications related to prey choice and foraging strategy.

Although this project was planned for three years, almost all the chicks at the Jackson Head colony appeared to have been killed by stoats during the 2016 breeding season.

A 2017 survey by BirdLife International suggested a population of between 5,000–7,000 mature birds, but the problem of finding them makes it difficult to reach conclusions about population trends. Some believe that the population has been in decline, but sightings by the DOC, boat skippers and the Tawaki Project in Milford Sound since 1991 suggest that numbers there have shown a significant improvement from a low-point in the 1950s.

When some birds were found for the first time breeding on the Otago coast in 2015 there was some hope that the overall population trend might be moving upwards. In 2019 the total population was calculated at between 2,500–3,000 breeding pairs, but for the reasons outlined above this was an estimate only.

Grey Warbler

Order:	Passeriformes
Family:	Acanthizidae
Scientific name:	*Gerygone igata*
Other names:	riroriro, rainbird, teetum, New Zealand gerygone, grey gerygone
New Zealand status:	Endemic
Conservation status:	Not threatened

In 2007 this vocally exuberant bird was voted by popular choice as New Zealand's Bird the Year. It is closely related to other members of the *Gerygone* genus found throughout Australasia and South-East Asia and was first described by John Gray of the *Erebus* and *Terror* Expedition in the early 1840s.

It readily adapted to Maori and early European settlement and Maori celebrated it during their Matariki celebration of the New Year, which is about the eventual return of summer and the need to prepare to plant new crops.

The Grey Warbler is one of the most widely distributed of New Zealand's endemic birds and it can be found the length and the breadth of the country. Walter Buller wrote: 'In the warm of the sunlight of the advancing summer, when the manuka is covered with its snow-white blossoms, the air is laden with the fragrance of forest flowers, admit the happy hum of insect-life, a soft trill of peculiar sweetness – like the chirping of a merry insect – falls upon the air, and presently the tiny bird appears for an instant in the topmost twigs of some low bush, hovers for a few moments,

Grey Warbler. Shutterstock/Imogen Warren

like a moth before a flower, or turns a summersault in the air, then drops out of sight again. This is the grey warbler, the well-known riroriro of Maori history and song.'

Shining Bronze-Cuckoo.
Shutterstock/Imogen Warren

Weighing just 6g it's a small bird, but it has a distinctive trilling call and typically hunts for insects in the canopies or woody shrubs and trees. A Landcare Research New Zealand study between 2007–15, involving thousands of home gardens, discovered that the Grey Warbler frequents 25 per cent of all domestic gardens in New Zealand from the North Cape to Bluff. Further work by Landcare, working in association with the University of Auckland, proved that it is more likely to inhabit rural rather than urban gardens, in places where the owners do not feed common species such as sparrows because these will displace it by more than 50 per cent.

The Grey Warbler can often be seen flying short distances, moving between branches in the canopy. It usually forms pairs, where contact is maintained with short *chip* calls. Pairs will stay in their territory year-round but will not defend this outside the breeding season.

They will almost hover to feed on caterpillars, flies, beetles, moths, spiders and other small invertebrates at the ends of leaves and twigs, and are the only birds in New Zealand that will often glean insects from the outside of the canopy while hovering. This distinctive behaviour makes them identifiable from far off. They will occasionally join flocks of other insectivorous birds such as Silvereyes, Brown Creepers and Whiteheads.

The maximum dispersal distance for each bird is up to 3km and its lifespan is up to five years. The Grey Warbler is unique among the birds of mainland New Zealand in that it builds an enclosed suspended nest. In the North Island it appears to have only one clutch per season, while birds in the South Island will typically have two. In all cases 3–5 eggs are laid.

The species is host to the brood-parasitic Shining Bronze-Cuckoo. The female cuckoo will remove a single egg from the warbler's nest and replace it with one of her own. The warbler nestlings have a high-pitched begging call which the cuckoo chick will mimic while in the nest and as a dependent fledging and the warbler seems to accept this. After hatching, the cuckoo chick will eject the other eggs and any nestlings from the nest and be raised alone.

Kakapo

Order:	Psittaciformes
Family:	Strigopidae
Scientific name:	*Strigops habroptilus*
Other names:	night parrot, owl parrot, Tarepo
New Zealand status:	Endemic
Conservation status:	Nationally Critical and recognised in New Zealand as a taonga
Other information:	2008 New Zealand Bird of the Year

Kakapo stamp.
New Zealand Post

With constant observation by radio and telemetry monitoring in the wild and video monitoring in the nest, the Kakapo remains one of if not the most highly managed species of bird in the world, and to the scientific world the most deviant parrot.

In 1883 Irish sawmiller, rabbitter, hunter and jack-of-all-trades Richard Henry settled at the southern end of Lake Te Anau where he built a small dwelling. He quickly became known as a bush guide and explorer and competed unsuccessfully with Quintin McKinnon in finding a route to the West Coast. In his spare time he observed, collected and preserved birds, often analysing the effects of weasels, stoats and ferrets.

Henry predicted the Kakapo's extinction and became a prolific writer criticising scientists' preference for formal analysis over field observations. During this time, he found a complete skeleton of a takahe close to his home in Patience Bay on the shore of Lake Te Anau. This can still be seen in the Otago Museum. It was also during this period that he found several Kakapo and described these in his writings.

In 1896 he noted: 'In less than half a century the bird will be extinct, unless the people of every country in the world realise their interest and value, then there will be no fear of them becoming extinct.'

After one memorable discussion with Professor Hutton, the curator of Canterbury Museum, Henry observed: 'He thinks more of a classical name than about a curious and wonderful fact. He seemed not at all interested in my story about kakapo but was very anxious to explain to me some straw-splitting difference that shifted a bird out of one class into another.'

After lobbying by Henry, Walter Buller and others, it was agreed that the presence of mustelids in the bush could wipe out entire bird populations in a matter of months. Powerful people stepped in and lobbied the New Zealand Department of Lands and Survey to establish a sanctuary in Dusky Sound in the Fiordland National Park. While the authorities were sceptical of Henry's wild ideas they nevertheless gave in and in 1894 appointed him the first caretaker of Resolution Island in Dusky Sound. This was the first wildlife reserve to be established in New Zealand and a landmark in New Zealand's conservation history.

After building a home and wharf on Resolution, he promptly set off with the help of his muzzled dog to find and begin transferring birds from the forested shoulders of the Sound to the island. He was so successful that by 1900 he had moved 700 birds, including many kiwi and kakapo, to Resolution Island and other islands in the sound such as Pigeon Island, thus achieving the first translocations of any wild birds anywhere in the world.

Over the next four years he prepared another 100 for shipping to reserves, government departments, botanical gardens, exhibitions, overseas museums and private persons. In doing so he pioneered capture techniques, experimented with dogs and nets, and proved that in the right conditions birds could survive relocation. During this time he also devoted nearly two years to searching for the South Island Takahe.

In March 1900 disaster struck when he learned that tourists on a boat had reported seeing a weasel on the shore of Resolution chasing a weka. In an effort to protect 'his'

Photo taken circa 1891 of Quintin McKinnon, the discoverer of the famous Milford Track, and his assistant Captain F.M. Duncan, showing a captive Kakapo standing on a ride pole by their camp and the carcasses of two Blue Ducks hanging from the upright centre pole. *The Encyclopaedia of New Zealand*

Richard Henry in front of his boatshed on Resolution Island. DOC

birds he transferred some to the smaller surrounding islands. For a year or two things seemed okay, but then small birds began to disappear from the sound and Kakapo became emaciated. Soon rats, mustelids, wild cats, hunting parties, fisherman and prospectors had begun to swamp him in his endeavours to protect the birds. When offered the job of ranger on Kapiti Island in 1908 he accepted; he left Dusky Sound in June that year at the age of 63 and took up the post on Kapiti Island, where he stayed until 1911 before returning to live on the mainland.

Between the late 1940s and the 1970s there were sporadic and decreasing numbers of Kakapo sightings but attempts to save the species continued, although increasingly extinction was looking like the most probable outcome. In the late 1950s Don Merton of the New Zealand Wildlife Service – later to become the DOC – was given the job of attempting to save the Kakapo. He was a keen advocate of many of Henry's theories and by the early 1970s was able to confirm that these worked and he was able to put them into practice.

Merton became a legend in the New Zealand conservation community. He not only saved the Kakapo, but also a number of native birds, including famously the Black Robin which is endemic to the Chatham Islands. To help pass on his knowledge and techniques he wrote or co-wrote more than 145 publications. By the time he died in April 2011 he had been awarded many honours and a doctorate in science.

The flightless nocturnal Kakapo, with its big voice and owl-like face, was probably one of the most common birds when the first humans arrived in New Zealand but is now one of the rarest in the world. It is the world's heaviest surviving parrot species and the world's only lek-breeding parrot. It is a large, capable solo hiker that runs along bush tracks cropping leaves. It is also a gentle, serious, warm, gregarious, endearing and very curious bird.

Due to a respiratory illness a Kakapo known as Sirocco had to be hand-raised as a chick and, in the process, became so well bonded with the DOC staff and researchers working with it that it became a nuisance. Despite the species not being known to swim, Sirocco became so attached to rangers on Whenua Hou that it went swimming with them. One day in frustration a ranger carried him to the far side of the island and set him down. He returned to find him standing on the doorstep.

Sirocco shot to international stardom on 18 March 2010 during the filming of the British Broadcasting Corporation documentary by Stephen Fry on endangered species called *Last Chance to See.* He was filmed trying to make love to an accompanying zoologist's hat. By 2017 he had 100,000 fans on his Facebook page.

Don Merton with Kakapo. DOC

While he is still a wild bird and lives in the wild, he prefers human company and as such has become recognised as a national treasure, a spokesbird for his species and an ambassador for endangered species.

Kakapo are solitary and do not form pairs. At around 1.5–2.5kg for a female and 2–4kg for a male it is the heaviest surviving species of parrot in the world and may be one of the longest lived, with a mean life expectancy of at least 60 years. The fossil bones of a much larger parrot, *Heracles inexpectatus*, were found by palaeontologists at the St Bathans site in Otago in July 2019; this bird is estimated to have stood up to 1m tall and weighed about 7kg.

The Kakapo's exceptionally soft moss-green and yellow feathers enable it to blend perfectly into the vegetation. It's almost impossible to see unless it moves and tends to freeze when feeling threatened. It is believed that this amazing camouflage evolved to protect it from aerial predators. It's a good climber and will often use its wings as climbing aids and to parachute back to the ground.

Kakapo feed on five-finger, hebes, wineberry, bush-lawyer, coprosma and other berry plants. They will only breed when the rimu trees produce large quantities of fruit.

Once occurring much more widely on both the North and South Islands, the Kakapo has a very distinctive and pleasant sweet scent. It's delicious flesh was much favoured by the South Island Nga Tahu Maori who hunted it in summer for its skin and feathers for fashioning into the fabric for the capes and cloaks of chiefs. By 1894 it had become very secretive, difficult to find and had retreated to the precipitous

Sirocco the Kakapo.

mountain valleys of Fiordland and other inhospitable places in the South Island.

Males go to extraordinary lengths to find and attract a breeding mate. As the male moves around its territory, it will establish well-defined pathways on spurs leading to the tops and along the ridges and will continually improve these by removing any intruding roots, fruit, or other impediments. These tracks can be as wide as 40–50cm and up to 200m long.

Where several males are present, they will establish their own tracks but together will expand the bower where the tracks meet into a 'ballroom' – known as a 'lek' – in the hope of attracting a mate. The males dig shallow scrapes, or bowls, connected to the tracks then, in summer, they will display in these by booming all night every night for 3–4 months.

While other birds around the world, such as cocks-of-the-rock, bowerbirds, some birds-of-paradise, manakins and grouse, create communal leks to dance and display, leks by Kakapo are solo efforts where bush is cleared to provide a sunspot and the background colour is manipulated to accent the bird's colourful plumage. Here, each bird will dance and display in its own lek, in the hope of attracting a female.

The male's booming mating call has been described as having a haunting, gut-stirring, vibrating, bass drum-like beauty, or being reminiscent of a foghorn! The bird uses its oesophagus to gulp in the air and then releases this in a booming belch. In

Fiordland one bird was recorded booming up to 1,000 times an hour for 17 hours. Such a huge effort means that the male will lose weight and condition during this process.

On hearing this throbbing low rhythmic boom, the female will respond by making her way to the lek to mate. The female's call has been compared to a crowing rooster or a squealing pig. Screaming *skraak* calls and donkey-like braying are associated with Kakapo territorial disputes.

The Kakapo's unusual lifestyle continues to excite many scientists around the world. It is believed that the shared lekking system is designed to ensure the female will mate with the most vigorous male, thus ensuring the long-term viability of the species. The fact that the highest incidence of pregnancy occurs when the lek is in full swing tends to support this theory, but research findings show that the most important factor is an abundance of nutrient-rich food which the flowers and fruit of the rimu tree provide.

In 1958 a private Kakapo aviary breeding facility was set up at Mount Bruce in the Wairarapa. This was achieved with the support of the Wildlife Service and in 1961 became the Pukaha Mount Bruce National Wildlife Centre. Breeding attempts continued there with eight birds until 1968, but not with the hoped-for success. Eventually the birds were transferred to the ecosanctuary known as Maud Island in Queen Charlotte Sound, which had been in existence for several years.

It was here that the male from the Gulliver Valley, the sole surviving stud male from the Fiordland population, was being held in a pen. He was to go on to become known as a symbol of hope for the species. Named 'Richard Henry' he went on to play a significant role by becoming the founding father in the renewal of his species by siring 51 chicks. When he died of natural causes in late December 2010 he may have been as much as 80 years old.

On 2 April 1974, the male Kakapo Jonathon and the female Jill, captured in the Esperance Valley in Fiordland, were transferred to Maud Island to join Richard Henry. It was only much later when Jill died that dissection of her body revealed she was in fact a male.

There was great excitement in 1980 when the first female Kakapo for 22 years, called Mandy, was caught on Stewart Island, then despondency two weeks later when she died. Fortunately, two weeks after this a second female named Maggie was caught on the island along with a male named Arab; both were transferred to Maud. Upon examining these two birds, Don Merton realised that the sexes could be told apart simply by taking a close look at their body weight and the markings on the trailing edges of their primary feathers – females are smaller and the mottling on the primary edges is different. Five years later the female Tara from Stewart Island was added to the population on Maud Island.

During the period 1973–1987 expeditions continued into many of the most rugged regions of Fiordland. These focussed on areas where the birds themselves had been seen or there was other evidence of their existence. These included the Tutoko Valley, various tributaries of the Cleddau River and the Esperance, Gulliver, Poseidon and Transit Valleys. Finally, a visit was made to the Sinbad Gully below Mitre Peak in the famed Milford Sound.

Map showing the location of Whenua Hou, or Codfish Island. Land Information New Zealand

While four of the birds captured in the 1980s survived, none were found in Fiordland. Only a male was found on Stewart Island, while 20–40 males and females were found on Whenua Hou and eight males and six females were found on the Little Barrier Island reserve established in the 1920s. The situation was declared critical, and the survival of the species was made one of the DOC's key priorities in terms money and other resources, which it remains today.

While Kakapo and stoats had coexisted on Maud Island for a few years in the 1990s in a regime with tight predator control, disaster struck when the female Tara was found mauled to death by a stoat. This resulted in the remaining birds being transferred to Whenua Hou, just off the Stewart Island coast.

In 1989 a further search of Fiordland failed to find any Kakapo, and just one was found on Stewart Island. This left just 65 Kakapo – 43 males and 22 females – on four offshore islands.

Early efforts at breeding were disappointing and with only 51 birds left in 1995 the DOC, New Zealand Aluminium Smelters (NZAS) and the Forest and Bird Protection Society established a Kakapo Recovery Programme whereby they agreed to work together. Nga Tahau Maori of the South Island undertook to support this work as their relationship with this species goes back centuries. This combined group soon became responsible for the decision-making processes around the protection, management and conservation of Kakapo. Within the first five years recovery was underway and the population increased to an estimated total of 62 birds.

One of the major problems is that while the males are keen to mate, only about 40 per cent produce fertile sperm, partially due to inbreeding.

During the period 1997–2005, 26 of the hand-reared chicks (62 per cent) were successfully returned to the wild. These had initially been kept in thermostatically controlled brooders, then in a conditioned room, and finally in a pen in an unheated room prior to transfer to an outdoor pen and later release into the wild. Incubation humidity was kept at 80 per cent to simulate that measured in Kakapo nests.

The growth rate of these youngsters was significantly slower than that of parent-reared chicks because most chicks were suffering from ill health or injury before being taken into captivity. During this time hand-reared Kakapo comprised 40 per cent of all chicks fledged since 1990 and by 2005 they comprised 20 per cent of the total population of 86 birds.

By now, as with some other threatened species, worldwide research was underway by molecular ecologists and other scientists to establish the Kakapo's genome sequence in the hope this would lead to improved breeding strategies, because only 65 per cent of eggs were found to be fertile. Researchers at Massey University used a gas chromatography spectrometer to analyse male sperm from those successful females who have produced fertile eggs. In the meantime artificial insemination, although costly and difficult to do in the wild, has proved successful.

Dr Jason Howard, a neuroscientist at Duke University in North Carolina, USA, had been reading his daughter a book about the Kakapo and became so charmed and intrigued by it that he sequenced the first complete genome. At this point the DOC set up a programme titled 'Kakapo 125,' at a cost of more than $100,000, to be crowdfunded through the Genetic Rescue Foundation of Massey University, which would be tasked with sequencing the genomes of the remaining birds.

On Whenua Hou all nests are monitored, eggs are removed and replaced with a dummy artificial egg which will encourage the female to mate again. Chicks are hatched in incubators then returned to the wild. Surplus eggs are removed, incubated, hand reared and then returned to the wild. There was excitement in 2015 when a chick was successfully hatched from a damaged egg recovered by the bird's human minders and held together with tape. This chick, named Lisa One, became an international celebrity.

In 2002 a Kakapo on Whenua Hou was found with an inflamed cloaca (the orifice from which urine and faeces are discharged). Rangers promptly named this mysterious condition 'Crusty Butt,' or cloacitis. As this illness can cause severe scabbing it can make the bird seriously ill, and as a result it has become a serious threat to the future of the species. There were more cases in 2013 and by 2019 at least 23 birds had been affected, resulting in at least one death. It is thought that unusually warm and humid weather on the island during the nesting period may have played a part. There has been a lot of ongoing work on how best to achieve prompt diagnosis to allow for early intervention. CT scans have helped to diagnose the condition, which is treated with antifungals and antibiotics, although once a bird has been diagnosed it can be a long road to recovery.

In 2012 nine Kakapo were translocated to Little Barrier Island in the Hauraki Gulf. It was estimated that it may take as long as 10 years before they could successfully raise their own chicks without support, but in February 2014 four eggs were found in two nests, of which two eggs were fertile. One of these was hatched on the island and the other was moved to Whenua Hou so that it wouldn't compete with its sibling for food.

In 2016 a bumper crop of the Kakapo's favourite fruit from the rimu tree resulted in 47 chicks, of which 34 fledged. As the mothers can usually only cope with one chick, DOC staff were left caring for nine of the youngsters. A temporary hand-rearing facility was established in Invercargill to facilitate this, and this offered a series of opportunities to view the fluffy white chicks, which proved irresistible to local people, many school groups and thousands of international tourists.

In April 2019 the fungal disease aspergillosis was first diagnosed in 20 Kakapo on Whenua Hou. This respiratory infection is a noncontagious relatively common disease in caged and domestic birds, but not so frequently found in free-living birds. Unfortunately it is difficult to diagnose in the early stages when treatment with antimicrobials could help.

The best Kakapo breeding season on record at the time of writing was in 2019 when two eggs were laid by each of the 49 females. This meant that, despite the deaths of two adult females and three chicks due to aspergillosis, the population increased to 208 birds. Nearly 50 Kakapo were transferred from Whenua Hou to veterinary hospitals for testing and treatment for aspergillosis as well as other medical conditions. Kakapo at the other predator-free island sanctuaries were reported as fine.

The same year a breakthrough was made when three female Kakapo were successfully inseminated artificially, and two chicks were hatched. This was the first time that artificial insemination had been successful in Kakapo.

In 2019 consideration was being given to a less direct approach to management by relocating genetically diverse Kakapo populations to suitable habitats where the species was once common, such as Sinbad Gully in Fiordland. This would provide an opportunity to develop separate populations within an agreed genetic range. While Sinbad Gully is an exceedingly difficult-to-penetrate mountain enclave protected by near-vertical rock walls hundreds of metres high it is possible, given time, that stoats may breach this fortress.

Kaka

Order:	Psittaciformes
Family:	Strigopidae
Scientific name:	*Nestor meridonalis*
Other names:	bush parrot, brown parrot, kawkaw
New Zealand status:	Endemic
Conservation status:	Recovering

The Kaka is generally heard before it is seen and can be found on both the South and North Islands, although its range has been much reduced due to forest clearance and browsing by introduced mammals. Its preference for a wide variety of forest types, including podocarps and beech forests, means it has an important role to play in pollinating many native plants.

Many confuse it with the Kea, which is larger, has olive-green plumage and is confined to the South Island. Typically the female Kaka's plumage is paler than that of the male. These birds weigh 475–575g and in general there is an incremental increase in size from north to south. While North Island and South Island subspecies are recognised this is not supported by genetic data.

Kaka. Shutterstock/Martin Pelanek

Its voice is a harsh repeated *ka-aa* when flying above the forest canopy, a grating *kraak* alarm when disturbed and it has a variety of loud musical whistles which vary markedly from place to place. Males give a soft *tsee-twee-tsee* call when showing potential nest sites to females, while females soliciting food from their mates and juveniles soliciting food from their parents utter a guttural repeated *aa-aa* call.

The Kaka is a very capable flyer and can weave its way among tree trunks and branches. When flying long distances, it tends to travel in groups of three or more and fly at a slow methodical speed in a direct course. It has been known to fly 15–20km in less than 30 minutes. When on the ground it normally hops along.

Kaka congregate in groups at localised feeding points such as flowering rata but will often forage for wood-boring larvae, fruit, seeds, nectar, sap and honeydew, for which it will use its brush-fringed tongue. When alone it will usually remain silent and the only sound to betray its presence is the soft sound of falling wood chips or seed fragments as it forages. Its breeding range varies from 1.5–2km, while non-breeding birds may travel up to 5–10km in their home valley.

Early Maori regarded it as rangatira (chief of all birds). As such its feathers were highly prized for cloaks and elements for display on war canoes, weapons and important tools. It was believed these added strength and power. Kaka were trained to act as decoys on their bird-feeding troughs, which were used to snare and spear Kaka and Kereru.

Kaka were also kept as pets and taught to talk and do other tricks; some were taught to speak Maori to welcome visitors. The bird was seen in most villages, where it would be secured to its domestic perch by a beautifully crafted greenstone leg ring. Highly prized, some were kept in cages of greatest mana (respect); these were made from the bones of tribal ancestors.

As the Kaka was once an abundant forest dweller it was much favoured by Maori who, while they regarded it as the most important bird of the forest, ate it as enthusiastically as they did Kereru, and claimed it was best eaten after being preserved.

For some reason there was a short supply of its food on the West Coast in 1856, so Kaka took to raiding the barns and stacks of the settlers who, upset by this behaviour, shot them by the hundreds.

Writing in 1875 Buller observed: 'It is sprightly in its actions, eminently social, and noisier than any other inhabitant of the woods, and every morning will wake the weary traveller in the bush.' In June that year he recorded that a Captain Main, when out hunting, had reported seeing some Kaka that were so fat they could not fly and had caught 15 on the ground. In the 1880s during a two-hour Maori versus European Kaka-hunting competition, with two hunters on each side, Maori took 150 birds using their traditional methods while the Europeans took 100 with their guns.

The Kaka has become a common sight in the Wellington city green belt, having spread from the Zealandia Ecosanctuary in nearby Karori. As it can do impressive damage to trees using its hooked upper mandible and lower bill, barking a tree in search of grubs or insects, the city council has responded by planting species it dislikes.

While it has been estimated that there are probably fewer than 10,000 Kaka left, there appears to be sufficient gene flow between populations to prevent the development of significant genetic differences between them. Importantly, it is one of the few species that can coexist with rats and possibly with possums, although it cannot cope with stoats.

Kea

Order:	Psittaciformes
Family:	Strigopidae
Scientific name:	*Nestor notabilis*
Other names:	New Zealand mountain clown, mountain parrot
New Zealand status:	Endemic
Conservation status:	Nationally endangered
Other information:	2017 New Zealand Bird of the Year

The range of this monogamous bird is now restricted to alpine areas of the South Island high country from Fiordland to Nelson and Marlborough, where it favours high-altitude beech forests and open subalpine herb fields. It breeds almost exclusively at altitudes over 750m above sea level. It is well known and mostly enjoyed by those who congregate in the South Island's ski resorts, alpine tourist spots, mountain huts and alpine passes.

The Kea can fly long distances and birds it may travel down to sea level. They can live for up to 80 years in captivity but have a life expectancy of only 20 years in the wild. Males stay together in groups until reaching breeding age at around three years.

Fossil remains from a cave near Waikato indicate that this large colourful bird, which is the world's only true alpine parrot, was in New Zealand 18,000 years ago.

Kea. Shutterstock/Robert L Sanson

Kea habitat.

At this time it was probably widespread in what today are North and South Islands, although then they may have been connected by a land bridge.

As the Kea only has a few taste pits on its tongue it can only select food on the basis of shape, size and colour, rather than taste and smell, so a young bird will learn what's good to eat by chewing on everything and has an innate fascination for unusual objects including vehicle wiper blades, rubber sealing strips and lead. As a consequence, they think lead is a yummy treat and will hunt it from all sorts of sources including bullets, nails, flashing on houses and rubbish bins. Many will die, as lead is one of the most toxic metals in the world.

Parrots and crows are the brainiest members of the bird world and Kea, like Kaka, regularly excels at intelligence tests. It's a good problem solver and has an irresistible sense of play and curiosity. Unwary trampers and mountaineers have often fallen foul of it investigating the contents of their packs or stealing their bootlaces, while it may ruin abandoned tents. It's also a keen scrounger of food scraps and will even steal food from unwary humans.

Sir Charles Fleming, the distinguished New Zealand scientist and ornithologist, once rescued an unattended Kea chick from high in the Southern Alps and took it home for his wife Molly, where it proved to be a constant source of fun. In her subsequent book *A Kea on My Bed* she wrote: 'What he most wanted to know was how things worked, and he would pull corks out of bottles then try to put them back,

Kea scrounging food from tourists.

or prise the lids from tins, playing all kinds of football with them and rolling them around the room.'

The explorer and mountaineer Arthur Paul Harper, or APH as he liked to be called, observed: 'The Keas, having settled on the ice, began to follow in a long straggling line, about 15 of them. They have a predatory solemn walk, but when in a hurry they hop along on both feet, looking very eager and very much in earnest. To judge from their expressions, they were in a great state of anxiety. Now and then the one in front would turn around and shriek *ke-aaa* as much as to say: 'It's all right boys, come along.''

Kea nest at the end of a long tunnel, in crevices among rocks, or in the hollows of root systems of old trees. Many of these sites will be in a well-drained slip of moraine debris in the upper reaches of beech forest and nests are always cleaned out and rebuilt the following year.

Prior to European arrival it probably fed on the carcases of dead or dying moa, but it was quick to adapt to alternatives. By the 1860s high-country farmers claimed it was killing many sheep by standing on their backs in winter and feeding on their kidneys and fat. The farmers may well have encouraged this as they would leave the green pelts of butchered sheep killed for meat hanging on fences wool-side down. Careless work exposed any remaining fat and flesh and proved to be an irresistible temptation to the hungry birds.

Sign for tourists at Arthur's Pass.

The government responded by issuing a bounty of two shillings and two pence for a Kea beak, which eventually rose to one pound. That was a lot of money at the time and it has been estimated this scheme resulted in the death of 150,000 Kea.

By 1907 people were beginning to have doubts about the accuracy of the perceived threat, and the theory was challenged and the law overturned. To protect the survivors, killing them was outlawed in 1970. By this time only an estimated 4,000 or so Kea remained.

In 1986 the Minister of Internal Affairs announced: 'Now is the time to pass legislation, now is the time to rescue the declining birds, rather than waiting until they reach the brink of extinction.'

In 2009 only 2 per cent of the Kea nests in Kahurangi National Park in Nelson produced young without predator control. In 2011 a 1080 poison operation was carried out there by OSPRI as part of its tuberculosis-free programme to protect dairy herds from bovine tuberculosis spread by possums. This programme was continued in 2014 and 2015–16. At the close of the 2015–16 breeding season research revealed that on average 50 per cent of the monitored nests produced young.

While this mountain clown can suffer from viral diseases, staphylococcal infections, scouring from food poisoning and a wide variety of parasites including mites, lice, internal threadworms and kea fleas, the greatest threat to it at present is probably excessive attention from tourists.

Kiwi

These strange and wonderful birds evolved to fill ecological niches in terms of habitat and lifestyle that in most other places in the world would be occupied by mammals.

Old kiwi stamp.
New Zealand Post

During a visit to New Zealand the great conservationist Sir David Attenborough said of the kiwi: 'It is arguably even more extraordinary than the moa itself.' Like the moa, many researchers in ornithology want to study kiwi as DNA sequencing is revolutionising its status in terms of taxonomy (the science of identifying new species and relationships between species).

The kiwi is New Zealand's national bird and regarded as taonga (a treasured possession) by Maori who have a strong cultural and historic association with it, for example kiwi feathers are valued for weaving soft cloaks for people of high rank. For these reasons Maori play a key role in its protection and conservation. They have put it under the protection of their god Tane, and call it 'Te Manu a Tane,' the bird that Tane hid. Only the most important Maori of great mana are allowed to wear a kiwi-feather cloak.

The first kiwi specimen collected by Europeans appears to be a Southern Brown Kiwi which arrived in England around 1812. The skin of this bird, currently held at the World Museum in Liverpool, formed the basis for the official description of the species as *Apteryx australis*, meaning 'southern wingless bird.' The first published illustration of a kiwi, based on the same bird, was a hand-coloured engraved illustration by Richard Nodder that appeared in the 1813 edition of George Shaw and Elizabeth Nodder's *The Naturalist's Miscellany*. As the drawing was made from a kiwi skin the illustration gave the bird an elongated appearance. On 1 May 1846, the explorer Dumont D'Urville asked a Maori to find him a kiwi, whereupon for a small fee he was presented with a pair.

Since 1861 the kiwi has periodically featured as the logos of some of New Zealand's companies, on many issues of its coins and postal stamps, and is used as a trademark. It often appears in newpapers, magazines and on TV, forms the central image of the rondels on aircraft of the Royal New Zealand Air Force and features heavily in the country's tourism material. The bird is entwined in the identity of New Zealand citizens who since 1918 have become widely known throughout the world as 'Kiwis.'

While many New Zealand residents have probably seen a mounted kiwi in a

Kiwi on advertising material.

museum, fewer would have seen a live example of these predominantly nocturnal birds in any of the 11 ecosanctuaries in the North Island or four in the South Island where some species can be viewed. Furthermore, apart from conservation staff and volunteers, and avid birdwatchers, very few people indeed would have seen a kiwi in the wild. However, almost everyone has heard about it or read something about it somewhere; it's sometimes referred to as the peoples' bird.

Recent DNA work and molecular genetic evidence suggests that the distant ancestors of these ultimate probing birds flew, swam or island-hopped to their present locations as the survivors of the mass extinction of species around 65 million years ago.

Members of the Palaeognathae superorder have a palate resembling that of reptiles, while many have a flat sternum, usually without a keel, which makes them either unable to fly or at best poor flyers. Species of flightless birds belonging to this group are known as ratites, thus kiwi are related to the extinct giant elephant birds of Madagascar, the African ostriches, South American rheas and the Australasian cassowaries and emus.

Kiwi are also related to moa, and through this family to the tinamous of Central and South America. Prior to the Holocene Period New Zealand may have supported 16–17 lineages of kiwi, of which only one is still extant. Today all five species of kiwi currently recognised are classified in the single genus *Apteryx*. While scientists continue to investigate the DNA of these birds the mystery of their origins may well have more twists and turns.

Kiwi rondel on RNZAF aircraft.

It has been estimated, from fossil records found throughout the North and South Islands, that before the arrival of humans, when forests covered 70 per cent of the land, the kiwi population may have been as high as 12 million birds.

To survive the destruction of its prime

habitat by arriving humans, remnant populations of kiwi adapted to inhabit regenerating scrub, swamp and farm pasture from sea level to alpine level. Some species are known to disperse up to 22km in search of suitable habitat.

While Maori have historically hunted kiwi, this was done in season and with strict rules to prevent overexploiting the population. To help hunt it they used the Kuri (Maori dog) fitted

Kiwi crossing warning sign.
Shutterstock/Lakeview Images

with a rattle of wood, shells or bone, and usually with a muzzle. Few dogs were ever reported as missing or running loose in the bush. It was roasted over an open fire, steamed in a ground oven (umu), or boiled, but its flesh was regarded as inferior to that of the kereru. For storage or transport it was cooked in its own fat.

Kiwi are a flightless wonder and one of legend and folklore. Unlike other birds they have hair-like plumage but no tail, wings that are so small as to be virtually hidden and useless, long whiskers like a cat, a strong sense of smell and touch, marrow-filled bones, large ear openings and a blood temperature of 37–38°C. They also produce large eggs which hatch into independent chicks. The exceptionally long bill is used to probe deeply into leaf litter and soil on the forest floor in search of small invertebrates, with the birds favouring earthworms and the larvae of beetles, cicadas and moths. They will also eat centipedes, spiders, crickets, weta, small fallen fruit and leaves.

Kiwi nostrils are located along both sides of the tip and upper bill in a honeycomb-like structure, while both the inside and outside of the mouth are richly endowed with sensory nerve pits. While hunting a kiwi will continuously emit a snuffling sound and will always touch anything it finds with the tip of its bill. If captured it will spend a long time exploring the limits of its surroundings with the tip of its bill.

In 1835 the Anglican missionary William Yates described kiwi flesh as: 'Black, sinewy, tough and tasteless.' The missionary Richard Taylor described it as: 'Good eating, and tastes like tender beef rather than bird. The principal fleshy parts are the ribs and legs.'

Except for the Stewart Island Tokoeka, which can sometimes be seen during the daytime and evening, other kiwi are nocturnal and emerge shortly after nightfall. They are the only birds in the world to roost year-round and nest in a burrow, hollow tree or log, or under thick vegetation.

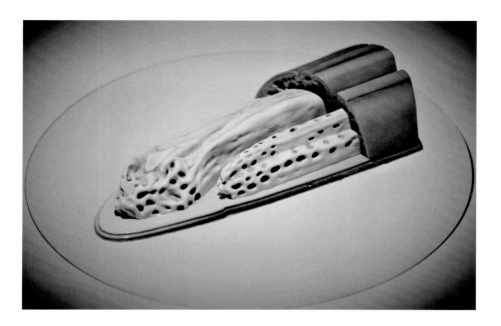

Sensory nerve pits in the kiwi bill.

Kiwi are usually heard rather than seen. Males give a repeated high-pitched ascending whistle while females give a deeper throaty cry. These calls are usually to advertise territory or maintain contact with partners. Pairs will often duet with the partner responding a few seconds after the first call.

Both the male and female make a practise of sniffing around their territory. A male can have up to 40 burrows in a territory and a female as many as 50. Burrows are concealed in thick vegetation or under the buttresses of tree roots or fallen logs. Kiwi are also thought to mark their territory or stake its claim, much as a cat does, by rubbing against a log.

Kiwi have small eyes and poor vision and compensate for this with exceptionally good senses of hearing and smell. The large brain relative to the bird's size allows it to process the large amounts of input data received through its ears and the neural receptors in the front 5mm of its bill.

When Walter Buller was introduced to kiwi by local Maori, they assured him the birds were common in many places. He wrote: 'They go about in companies of six to twelve, and make the country resound at night with their shrill cry.' A kiwi will sometimes share its favourite roosting sites, but this behaviour is more common during the breeding season and is thought to be associated with finding a mate.

Kiwi have strong and powerful legs, can run as fast as a person, and are gritty, feisty, strident, aggressive, and used to hard knocks. They are also strongly territorial and will fight to the death to hold on to a territory; these jump-and-slash affairs often result in fatal injuries. At least one species is a good swimmer. Using its claws, a kiwi can negotiate very steep slopes.

Kiwi are mostly monogamous with partnerships known to last 20 years. The breeding season runs from July through to December. The mating ritual has been historically recorded as the male rolling, leaping, hopping and even lying on its back kicking its feet together, with the female positioning herself to aid penetration and prevent the male falling off her back. In some instances, the male has been observed doing a lot of chasing and feet clicking while the female seems disinterested. Other instances have been observed of the female soliciting attention.

The female digs or scoops out a nesting place then deposits her egg, after which she may abandon her mate and sometimes pair with another male to form another nest. For his part the male attends to incubation and will feed and tend the chick until it can look after itself.

Normally one or two large eggs are laid in each nest. The size makes them too difficult for small mammals to successfully attack. When it is ready to hatch the chick will call from inside the egg. It will then heave and flex itself to crack the shell. When this is achieved it will poke its bill out to breathe, then use its feet to break up the egg and emerge as a tiny replica of its parents. The newly hatched chick has an external sac of egg yolk that can last for ten days.

Kiwi have an estimated lifespan of 40 years in the wild, but without intensive management 19 out of 20 chicks will not survive for more than a year. These birds have disappeared from many lowland sites around the fringes of its original distribution areas due to habitat loss and predation by dogs, ferrets and stoats. In many areas landscape-scale periodic aerial 1080 operations or trapping has slowed or reversed this decline.

In 2018 the DOC estimated the total population for all species of kiwi to be 63,500 – that's a 99 per cent reduction since the 1920s. It's estimated that 27 kiwi are killed each week. That's an annual loss of 1,404 birds. While 50–60 per cent of young kiwi survive in locations where management takes place, without such management 95 per cent die before reaching breeding age. A chick survival rate of 20 per cent is needed to ensure population increase. A sustainable population requires a minimum of 10 per cent of chicks to survive for six months. Once they weigh about 1.2kg the chicks can defend themselves against all predators excepting dogs. A single roaming dog can wipe out an entire population in a few days.

North Island Brown Kiwi

Order:	Apterygiformes
Family:	Apterygidae
Scientific name:	*Apteryx mantelli*
Other names:	Northern brown kiwi, kiwi kura, kiwi nui
New Zealand status:	Endemic
Conservation status:	Declining, the rate varying across the five different regional populations

This is probably the most abundant species of kiwi, with a population of about 25,000 birds. Five isolated populations are found around North Island. It occurs in native and exotic forests, scrub and rough farmland in Northland, although some populations have been decimated by dogs. It is also found north of the Manawatu, around southern Hawke's Bay and at Remutaka Forest Park near Wellington where a monitored population of 30 birds has resulted in good population growth. The initial monitoring from 2006–11 was carried out using radio-tracking of birds carrying transmitters and showed only limited spread from their release site.

North Island Brown Kiwi. Shutterstock/Lakeview Images

The Remutaka population has grown with time and has been helped by Operation Nest Egg. In 2011 acoustic monitoring was introduced as the increase in numbers had made it difficult to monitor the birds using radio-tracking. By 2018, 30 recorders were used, each positioned 400m apart. By 2019 the population had grown to more than 100 birds and the acoustic monitoring documented a slow spread from the release site as the number of birds increased.

North Island Brown Kiwi usually lays two eggs per season but may lay another two. It has been known for a pair to raise four chicks in one season. Each egg will be equal to 20 per cent of the bird's body weight – that's 430g per egg.

All public roads in sites where wild kiwi are known to exist are clearly marked with road signs asking motorists to exercise care. Dog owners near these areas are notified of the protected status of these birds and warned that it is an offence under law to take a dog into or near kiwi habitat. They are offered free kiwi-aversion training for their dogs if required.

Southern Brown Kiwi

Order:	Apterygiformes
Family:	Apterygidae
Scientific name:	*Apteryx australis*
Other names:	Southern Tokoeka, Fiordland Tokoeka, South Island Brown Kiwi
New Zealand status:	Endemic
Conservation status:	Threatened/nationally vulnerable

Two subspecies are formally recognised, these being: Fiordland Tokoeka, *A.a. austalis*; and Stewart Island Tokoeka, *A.a. lawryi*. Both are classified as threatened/nationally vulnerable. A third form, the Haast Tokoeka, *A.a.* 'haast', is recognised as distinct by some and is also classified as threatened/nationally vulnerable.

Due to habitat loss and predation the number of Fiordland birds has undergone a dramatic decline and the species has all but disappeared from northern and eastern Fiordland. There are thought to be only 250–300 birds remaining on the mainland, although a landscape-scale stoat-trapping programme appears to have halted or is

Fiordland Tokoeka, *A.a. austalis.* Shutterstock/Allan Pritchard

Stewart Island Tokoeka, *A.a. lawryi*. In 2018 the population was thought to be around 13,000 birds. Shutterstock/Vee Snijders

perhaps reversing the decline. New populations have been established on predator-free islands and in total the population is thought to number about 12,000 birds.

The Stewart Island subspecies was first described by Walter Lawry Buller and hence named after him as the Stewart Island Tokoeka, *A.a. lawryi*. Somewhat surprisingly Buller had an ambivalent attitude towards the conservation of rare species. His attitude was to collect the few remaining specimens while he could. Unlike other forms of kiwi, this bird is the only one of its kind that can often be found foraging during the daytime and evening.

The shy and reclusive mountain-loving Haast Tokoeka is found in the precipitous, tough, subalpine forest behind the township of Haast on the West Coast. With only about 400 birds left it is the rarest of all kiwi taxa.

Okarito Brown Kiwi

Order:	Apterygiformes
Family:	Apterygidae
Scientific names:	*Apteryx rowi*
Other names:	rowi
New Zealand status:	Endemic
Conservation Status:	Critically endangered. In 2019 the population was estimated to be around 600 birds.

Okarito Brown kiwi stamp. New Zealand Post

The only wild population is found in the Okarito forest on the South Island West Coast where each bird needs a territory of 100 hectares. This is the largest required by any kiwi species.

A captive-breeding programme for this bird and the Haast Tokoeka (*Apteryx australis* 'Haast') has been established in the township of Franz Josef. This, the West Coast Wildlife Centre, was established as a joint partnership between private enterprise and the Department of Conservation. It is the largest such facility in the country, is open to the public, and is playing a significant role in saving the species from extinction.

Before 2002, when the distinctiveness of this species was recognised, a substantial portion of this forest had been logged in the 1950s. Since 2002 an 11,000-hectare sanctuary has been created in the forest and considerable efforts have been made to increase kiwi numbers through pest control and the removal of eggs for hatching in captivity.

There were only 160 birds in 1995. Following the implementation of more intensive predator control, and with the support of Operation Nest Egg, the population rose to 375 in 2017 and to 675 in 2019. As the Okarito Forest has now reached capacity other breeding populations have been established, with one at Lake Gault near Fox Glacier. In 2020, 500 birds were counted but the species is still seldom seen without an experienced guide.

Road running through Okarito Brown Kiwi habitat.
Shutterstock/Lakeview Images

Great Spotted Kiwi

Order:	Apterygiformes
Family:	Apterygidae
Scientific name:	*Apteryx haastii*
Other names:	roa, roroa, roa-roa
New Zealand status:	Endemic
Conservation status:	Threatened. Population estimated at 13,000 in 2018

Measuring nearly half a metre in length, this is the largest of all kiwi and it has a population of around 13,000 birds in the north-west of the South Island. It is more robust, has a much more powerful bill and larger blackish feet than any other kiwi. It is also difficult to find in the rugged mixed podocarp forests which it favours in a range that incorporates the western side of the Southern Alps from Arthur's Pass to Kahurangi National Park in the far north of the West Coast.

Great Spotted Kiwi. Shutterstock/Lakeview Images

Little Spotted Kiwi

Order:	Apterygiformes
Family:	Apterygidae
Scientific name:	*Apteryx owenii*
Other names	kiwi pukupuku, grey kiwi
New Zealand status:	Endemic
Conservation status:	Recovering

This is the smallest kiwi species. With a depressing nesting success rate of 0.08 chicks per year in the wild it can now be found only in predator-free sanctuaries.

It was saved from extinction by the translocation of five birds from Jackson Bay on the West Coast to Kapiti Island in 1912. Unlike other kiwi species it only nests from October to February and it usually produces just one egg. Even the adults are too small to withstand a stoat attack.

From the Kapiti population another seven healthy populations have been established in predator-free sanctuaries and offshore islands, but a genetic bottleneck exists. Scientists are seeking solutions by using a host of modern technologies to better understand its genetic structure, and by using genetic analysis techniques to improve genetic diversity. The information gained from these strategies is allowing new management techniques to be used. This is improving nesting success and population numbers are growing.

At 300g the eggs of this kiwi are huge relative to the size of the female, which weighs 1.3kg.

Little Spotted Kiwi. Shutterstock/John Carnemolla

Kiwi with eggs.

Skeleton kiwi with egg.

New Zealand Dabchick

Order:	Podicipediformes
Family:	Podicipedidae
Scientific name:	*Poliocephalus rufopectus*
Other names:	New Zealand grebe, weweia, totokipio, taihoropi (in Hokianga), taratimoho (in Waikato)
New Zealand status:	Endemic
Conservation status:	Recovering

This, shy, secretive aquatic bird, which measures 29cm and weighs 250g, occurs predominantly on the North Island, having become extinct on South Island, perhaps due to pressure from introduced predators. However, a pair was found breeding near Takaka in Nelson in 2012, and another pair was seen near Blenheim in 2015, so it may return to some of its former haunts.

On North Island it can be seen on lakes, ponds, dams and oxidation ponds, but it is most common in the sand-dune lakes of the Central Volcanic Plateau. New Zealand Dabchicks migrate by night in search of new lakes, favouring high-quality wetland habitats that are buffered from the effects of surrounding land management and surrounded by dense riparian cover.

These birds, like all grebes, have separate web-like lobes on each toe. This, and the fact that the legs are set far back on the body, make it an efficient underwater swimmer but mean that it has difficulty walking on land. These birds feed on small fish, crustaceans, tadpoles and insects such as water boatmen and their larvae. Due to its skulking nature and persistent diving for up to a minute at a time for food it is often missed by birdwatchers.

While usually silent, the New Zealand Dabchick sometimes calls at the nest with a shrill whistle and croak. The sexes are similar, and although measurements overlap, if the bird's bill is longer than 2.25cm its most likely to be a male.

The extended breeding season runs from June through to March with most clutches in September. Nests are well hidden in secure rafts of decomposing debris under cover of sheltering trees or raupo beds. Some nests can only be approached under water. The 2–3 eggs are incubated by both parents. Whenever the sitting bird leaves the nest of its own accord it will cover the eggs before doing so.

The chicks can dive and swim straight after hatching but are closely supervised by one or both parents until becoming independent at around 10 weeks. When young they are sometimes carried on the back of a parent, where they can be difficult to see. The young are fed fish, but the parents give them downy feathers to swallow as protection against the bones.

Walter Buller wrote of this species: 'It dives with amazing agility, and, entirely taken by surprise, will effectively dodge the gun by disappearing under the surface at the first flash, and before the discharge of shot has reached it.'

New Zealand Dabchick with chicks. Shutterstock/Imogen Warren

New Zealand Dotterel

Order:	Charadriiformes
Family:	Charadriidae
Scientific name:	*Charadrius obscurus*; northern subspecies *C.o. aquilonius*; southern subspecies *C.o. obscurus*; today these are split by some authorities as separate species
Other names:	tuturiwhatu, tutuniwhata, pukunui, kukuruatu, rako, red-breasted plover, New Zealand plover
New Zealand status:	Endemic
Conservation status:	northern subspecies: recovering; southern subspecies: threatened/nationally critical

This appealing squat-looking 25cm-long plover is one of the world's largest dotterels. The more common northern subspecies or species occurs mainly around coasts in the northern North Island, from Taranaki to North Cape in the west, and as far south as Mahia Peninsula in the east. In 2018 two birds were seen, and a nest was found, on the Kapiti Coast not far from Wellington. What was doubly remarkable was that this was the first breeding known so far south, and that the breeding area was subject to free-running dogs and considerable human foot traffic. The population is estimated to be about 1,600 birds.

The very rare southern subspecies or species has disappeared from most of South Island and can now only be found on Stewart Island and adjacent South Island coasts; its entire population may be as low as 40 individuals.

Although quiet beaches were once considered essential for breeding, the northern birds can now often be found close to residential areas and have nested on

New Zealand Dotterel.

motorway edges, sports grounds, the waste rock embankment of the Martha Gold Mine in Waihi, and on the Lakes Golf Course near Pauanui. They can also be found within the Auckland City area.

New Zealand Dotterel habitat.

The birds usually return to their breeding territories in August and will typically nest on low flat sites such as sandspits, sandy beaches, shell banks, dunes, tidal estuaries and river mouths where there is little or no vegetation. Here they may be joined by breeding Variable Oystercatchers and White-fronted Terns.

The nest is a simple scrape on the ground with little or no lining and can occasionally be found close to obvious objects such as pieces of driftwood or small clumps of vegetation. Theses nests are particularly vulnerable to high spring tides, storm surges, drifting sand, farm stock, human development and disturbance. Like most birds they are vulnerable to predators such as hedgehogs, stoats and rats, which commonly eat the eggs. Hedgehogs are the greatest threat as they can move up to 2km per night, eating eggs from nests along the way. If a clutch is lost for any reason a female may lay again up to four times.

When standing still the sandy plumage makes this bird difficult to see, but its habit of running quickly then pausing to feed often betrays its presence. It is approachable while feeding but will run quickly when disturbed. In a predator-free environment some birds have survived for 20 years or more; one individual is known to have lived for 42 years.

On hatching the chicks will run about and feed themselves, but it will take around 6–7 weeks before they can fly. The birds eat aquatic insects and terrestrial invertebrates such as sandhoppers, and may sometimes take small fish and crabs. One was recently seen eating the tips of glasswort plants – the first time such behaviour has been recorded.

Juveniles are known to wander widely, while many adults remain sedentary on their breeding grounds with most established pairs staying together for life.

New Zealand Dotterel is subject to a species recovery plan. The DOC and the Royal Forest and Bird Society of New Zealand have agreed to cooperate to manage 20–25 per cent of the population to ensure the species' survival. This will include nest monitoring and some captive breeding with release back into the wild.

New Zealand Falcon

Order:	Falconiformes
Family:	Falconidae
Scientific name:	*Falco novaeseelandiae*
Other names:	karearea, sparrow hawk, bush hawk, quail hawk
New Zealand status:	Endemic
Conservation status:	Recovering
Other information:	Elected New Zealand Bird of Year in 2012. Its image appears on the New Zealand $20 bank note

This is one of about 40 species in the genus *Falco* which are found around the world. With wings angled back it can shoot through the air like an arrow and is capable of reaching speeds of over 100km/hr. It can catch prey larger than itself, is one of New Zealand's most spectacular birds, and is also its most threatened bird of prey species.

Based on morphological and ecological differences three forms of this species are recognised. The small dark 'Bush falcon' lives in forests and is mainly found south of Hamilton and on the West Coast as far south as Greymouth. The larger and paler 'Eastern falcon' lives predominantly in drier open habitats east of the Southern Alps, but its range can extend from coast to coast in the central South Island. The 'Southern falcon' is of intermediate size and coloration and lives in Fiordland and on a few offshore Islands.

Early Maori used this bird to forecast the weather, saying: 'When a karearea screams in fine weather, next day there'll be rain; when it screams in rain, next day will be fine.'

Adult males weigh 240–350g and measure 40–50cm; females are larger at 410–720g. Chicks fledge at about five weeks.

New Zealand Falcons feed on live prey and hunt mainly by watching from a vantage point and making a fast direct attack, either grasping the target or striking it with both feet which are equipped with sharp talons. It can also surprise prey by contour-flying close to the ground. Late afternoon is often a favoured time for hunting. Prey includes mice, rats, hares, rabbits, large insects and, as proven by extensive research, introduced bird species.

The prey is often killed by a quick powerful bite to the back of the neck. The falcon then takes its victim to a plucking post where it plucks and consumes it. Around 16 hours later it will bring up the indigestible parts such as fur, feathers and bones in a pellet. This process will also clean its crop and bacteria from the walls of its crop.

Females can easily kill young rabbits and hares weighing up to 3kg. Both sexes will take large birds such as White-faced Herons, ducks and partridges, and they

New Zealand Falcon. Shutterstock/Robert L Sanson

also feed on insects such as grasshoppers and beetles.

Food plays an important role in falcon courtship, which starts in early spring when the male chases the female in spectacular swooping dives pretending to attack her. This is followed by aerial acrobatics and ends with the male offering her the prey he has caught.

Recently planted pine forests have become an important breeding habitat for bush falcons, with the highest density found in the huge Kaingaroa pine forest in the central North Island, where each bird's home range is around 9 square kilometres.

A New Zealand Falcon nest can be a scrape on the ground under a rocky outcrop, or in an epiphyte in an emergent forest tree. The clutch of 2–4 eggs takes about 33 days to hatch. Nestlings are fed by both parents, but the male does most of the hunting while the female guards the nest until the chicks fledge at around 31–45 days.

These birds are incredibly aggressive against all intruders at the nest. Instances have been recorded of females dive-bombing people 400m away. They are regarded as one of the worlds bravest, most aggressive falcon species, but surprisingly recent evidence suggests that they are not as successful in this role as expected against feral cats.

New Zealand Falcon.

Like many birds of prey in other countries, the growing number of wind turbines in New Zealand is presenting another threat to the survival of this falcon, as do power poles and lines. Despite being protected birds, when they are seen hunting hens or racing pigeons they are sometimes shot. Falcon eggs can also be taken by cats, hedgehogs, stoats, weasels, ferrets and rats, while dogs are a risk to chicks and adults.

A 1978 study estimated populations of 650 pairs of bush falcons in the North Island and the north-west coast of the South Island, 3,150 pairs of eastern falcons and 200 pairs of southern falcons. Given the species' conservation status and continuing problems with predators, it seems likely that the current population numbers may be lower.

Groups such as the Wingspan Bird of Prey Trust, Raptor Association of New Zealand and DOC have joined forces to save the birds by raising chicks in captivity and releasing them into the wild. Additionally, the Marlborough Winegrowers Association is supporting a breeding programme to re-establish falcons among the many vineyards on the Marlborough Plains in an effort to protect the ripening grapes from other avian species.

New Zealand Pigeon

Order:	Columbiformes
Family:	Columbidae
Scientific name:	*Hemiphaga novaeseelandiae*
Other names:	kereru, kuku, kukupa, native wood pigeon, wood pigeon, kokopa
New Zealand status:	Endemic
Conservation status:	Not threatened

While this bird is widespread and commonly found across New Zealand it is fully protected under the Country's Wildlife Act (1953). This is because the fate of this bird is crucial to the fate of many of the country's forests. Since the demise of moa, it's the sole surviving bird species capable of dispersing the large seeds from 70 different native plant species over long distances, including those of the karaka, miro, tawa and taraire.

Much to its detriment, the New Zealand Pigeon seems totally unafraid of humans, and while the population is classified as stable overall, the species is at risk of becoming locally extinct in areas such as Northland, Hawke's Bay and Marlborough due to the combined effects of predation, competition and in Northland unlawful hunting by young Maori. In other areas with good predator control the species is thriving. This is particularly so in the capital city of Wellington, where road signs warn motorists to be careful of low-flying kereru. Measuring 51cm and weighing 650g this is a big bird, and they can do serious damage to a car if they get hit!

The New Zealand Pigeon is quiet and reclusive by nature and can sometimes be seen sitting on a branch in the deep shade, quietly watching the watcher. It has earned the well-deserved reputation of being a glutton. Come springtime it is often seen guzzling on berries and will do anything, including hanging upside-down in a tree, to get a good feed.

If a pigeon eats too many berries it must sit in the sun to digest them. When the weather is warm the ripe fruit in its crop can ferment and turn to alcohol. In years when fruit is plentiful it has been known for pigeons to fall from trees, too drunk to perch. During this time it's not unusual for intoxicated birds to be taken to wildlife centres to sober up.

Like many long-lived birds, the New Zealand Pigeon breeds slowly. Studies have shown that in areas such as Northland fewer than 15 per cent of chicks survive long enough to become independent. If this decline continues in these areas, it may well become extinct there.

Mating usually occurs in spring or early summer and is preceded by spectacular aerial displays by both sexes, but more so by the male. Both will stall, dive, and even

New Zealand Pigeon.

loop the loop. Legend has it that the birds do this when drunk on puriri berries.

The female lays one egg which both adults brood during the 28-day incubation period. The female sits through the night and morning with the male taking over at noon until evening. The adult pigeons produce food for their chicks in the form of crop milk, which is a cottage cheese-like substance which is rich in protein. As the chicks grow, regurgitated food forms an increasingly larger part of the diet.

This bird was once hunted for its meat and feathers by Maori, either using a long wooden

Fairy and Plum Shooting Party, circa 1900. Courtesy Nelson Provincial Museum, Tyree Studio Collection: 176893

drinking trough fitted with a number of nooses, or with a spear. Some Maori iwi have been given permission by the DOC to use the feathers and bones of recovered dead birds for cultural purposes, and reports are sometimes received by the DOC of the bird being eaten for special occasions. While Maori valued Kereru and Kaka as important food sources and protected them accordingly a few European settlers took a different view.

Walter Buller noted: ' In its native country it is less esteemed for its beauty than it is as an article of food; and to Maori and colonists, in every part of New Zealand, pigeon shooting, at certain times of the year, offers an agreeable recreation, while for many it is a prelude to employment.'

Soon after this Maori realised this bird and kaka were some of the more important food sources, so seasonal hunting was introduced in order to conserve the populations and also to only hunt them at the time of the year when their flesh was most succulent.

New Zealand King Shag

Order:	Suliformes
Family:	Phalacrocoracidae
Scientific name:	*Leucocarbo carunculatus*
Other names:	king shag, kawau, New Zealand cormorant, rough-faced shag, Marlborough Sounds shag, Cook Strait cormorant
New Zealand status:	Endemic
Conservation status:	Nationally endangered

New Zealand King Shag. Shutterstock/Lisa Crawford

This bird is one the rarest in the world, and as such it is a prime target for international birdwatchers. For the last 246 years it has been confined to largely inaccessible sites in the outer Marlborough Sounds, from the west coast of D'Urville Island and east to where Queen Charlotte Sound and Cook Strait meet.

In May 1773, J.R. Forster collected one in Queen Charlotte Sound during Cook's second voyage to New Zealand. Subfossil deposits indicate it had occurred much earlier throughout the South Island.

This bird forages up to a depth of 25m and favours bottom-dwelling species such as flounder, leather jacket, blue cod, sea perch, red cod, red scorpionfish, pilchards, New Zealand sole, sandfish and spotty.

The New Zealand King Shag breeds in winter on low rock plateaus and on steep rock faces, with 80 per cent of the population nesting between 3–33m above mean high-tide level. Nests consist of a platform of sticks and seaweed cemented together with guano.

Clutches of 1–3 eggs are laid in May and June, and juveniles are present at colonies from July onwards. Both parents feed the chicks. Often the female arrives back at the colony around midday and the male then departs to forage. During the breeding season the bare skin on the face and throat changes colour to grey-blue.

A 2015 survey put the population at 839 birds. This included 187 pairs. A 2016 survey showed more than a 37 per cent decline in active breeding pairs in the space of just one year.

The restricted distribution and small numbers of this species mean that a single adverse event, such as an oil spill, could destroy most of the population. It is also vulnerable to the impact of toxic bloom in feeding sites, while its nests may be destroyed by major southerly storms. It is also vulnerable to human disturbance at its colonies and to set nets placed in close proximity to these.

On 4 February 2019 a five-year programme was established to better protect the species, which began with the banding of 11 juveniles and one adult. The group involved in the programme includes the Marine Farming Association and associated companies, Ngati Koata, Ngati Kuia, Fisheries New Zealand, Marlborough Regional Council and Wildlife Management International Ltd.

Nesting New Zealand King Shags. Shutterstock/Lisa Crawford

New Zealand parakeets

	Orange-fronted Parakeet	Yellow-crowned Parakeet
Order:	Psittaciformes	Psittaciformes
Family:	Psittacidae	Psittacidae
Scientific name:	*Cyanoramphus malherbi*	*Cyanoramphus auriceps*
Other names:	kakariki, Malherbe's Parakeet	kakariki
New Zealand status:	Endemic	Endemic
Conservation status:	Nationally threatened	Not threatened

Both the Yellow-crowned and Orange-fronted Parakeets belong to the genus *Cyanoramphus* and both were common in the 1800s when flocks would emerge from the forest to feed on grain and fruit crops. As a result, farmers and orchardists considered them to be pests and shot thousands in attempts to protect their crops. This culling, combined with the destruction of the birds' habitat, were the main reasons for their near demise.

The two species share the same bright green ground colour, except for some blue in primary feathers on the wing. The main difference is the Yellow-crowned has a yellow patch on the head, a red frontal band above the bill, and is a brighter green, while the Orange-fronted has a pale yellow patch on the head and an orange band above the bill.

The Yellow-crowned Parakeet can be found in the North and South Islands and prefers tall unbroken forest and scrub. It is never found in secondary or logged forest and is confined to subtropical and tropical forests and moist lowland podocarp forests from sea level up to 900m, where it is more likely seen following a season of heavy seed production.

Yellow-crowned Parakeet is one of the very few endemic birds in New Zealand that, with a DOC permit, can be held and bred in captivity by private owners. Their offspring are to be released into suitable approved predator-free wildlife sanctuaries such as Boundary Stream near Napier and Maungatautari Ecosanctuary. On occasion captive wild birds are fitted with transmitters to allow monitoring after release back into their natural environment and subsequent monitoring has shown that these birds have successfully produced chicks. Captured wild birds are also used to reintroduce some wild genes into the captive population.

The Orange-fronted Parakeet was first identified by the French Ornithologist Charles de Souance in 1857, possibly from a specimen collected in 1826 by Dumont D'Urville on his first voyage to New Zealand. It was only seen four times in the first half of the 20th century, then in the D'Urville Valley of Nelson Lakes National Park in 1965 and 15 years later in the Hope Valley, Canterbury. Since then four small populations have been located and some birds translocated to predator-free offshore

Yellow-crowned Parakeet.

islands. It remains the rarest of New Zealand's parakeets, although recent good news is that 151 Orange-fronted chicks were born in the wild in 2019, probably doubling the population to about 300 birds.

In February 2019, 15 Orange-fronted Parakeet chicks were banded in the South Branch of the Hurunui River in Arthur's Pass National Park, with the older ones fitted with transmitters to monitor their survival post fledging. During the same period, a released captive bird bred with a wild bird and produced a clutch of nine chicks.

Both species are strong flyers and can sometimes be seen flying high above the canopy. They are usually solitary or found in pairs but may form small flocks in autumn. In flight both species make a loud chatter that sounds like *ki-ki ki-kii* but

Orange-fronted Parakeet. Isaac Conservation and Wildlife Trust

they also have a range of quieter and less distinctive calls. Both feed on berries, seeds, fruit and insects, and in the absence of predators it's not unusual to see them foraging on the ground.

These parakeets usually breed between October and December and nest in holes in large trees up to 30m above the ground. They will breed in winter when food is abundant. The female incubates the 5–9 eggs for the 20 days until they hatch. During this time, the male will call her off the nest and feed her by regurgitation. On hatching, both parents feed the chicks. Birds of both species typically begin breeding at one year of age. Their longevity and maximum dispersal are unknown.

New Zealand Pipit

Order:	Passeriformes
Family:	Motacillidae
Scientific name:	*Anthus novaeseelandiae*
Other name:	pihoihoi, Australasian pipit
New Zealand status:	Endemic
Conservation status:	Declining

This small brown bird makes a sparrow-like *chirrup* and drawn-out *twee* call. It's similar to a skylark but unlike that species is loath to fly when disturbed. New Zealand Pipit is found in the North and South Islands, where it favours open barren desolate habitats from coast to alpine tops but avoids intensively farmed areas. It also likes shingle riverbeds, gravel roads, scree slopes and sandhills.

It feeds on open ground, eating insects and their larvae, small earthworms and occasionally small seeds. Breeding takes place from August–January. Usually 2–5 eggs are laid and the nest is always made in a depression on the ground and usually under the cover of grass, tussock, or clumps of rushes. In a good season two clutches are laid. These are incubated by the female for 14–15 days until hatching.

The young are fed by both parents until fledging after 14–16 days. Should the adults be disturbed during nesting the pair will take to the air – one will drop to the ground close to the nest, while the other will fly further off trying to draw away the intruder.

New Zealand Pipit appears to have been much more common in the past than it is today. Walter Buller wrote: 'They are always plentiful on the settlers' farmland and must be seen during the summer months perched in large parties on the roofs of the country houses or on the surrounding fences and buildings.' Today pipits are rarely seen except for in a few key areas.

New Zealand Pipit.

New Zealand robins

	North Island Robin	South Island Robin
Order:	Passeriformes	Passeriformes
Family:	Petroicidae	Petroicidae
Scientific name:	*Petroica longipes*	*Petroica australis*
Other names:	New Zealand robin, toutouwai, bush robin, miro	New Zealand robin, Kakariwai
New Zealand status:	Endemic	Endemic
Conservation status:	Declining	Declining

The South Island Robin and North Island Robin are larger and heavier than their cousin the New Zealand Tomtit, and have longer legs and a much more upright stance. Numbers of these noisy, active birds are being reduced steadily, predominantly by ship rats and stoats.

Both species are found in older native forests, tall scrub and older exotic plantations. In particular they favour locations where there is a dense closed canopy and plenty of ground litter for foraging. The North Island bird's stronghold is the central North Island while the South Island bird is probably most common in older forests and exotic plantations north of Fiordland and north of Arthur's Pass.

These robins favour damp areas, and the male will inhabit the same patch of forest – usually from 1–5 hectares – throughout its life. Unpaired males are great songsters and will sing loudly and often for up to 30 minutes at a time.

Both species are cautious but trusting around humans. In the early days of European settlement these birds were favourites of the lonely woodcutter, sharing his meals and hopping about at his feet. Now, in areas where walking tracks are used, the males will often become very confiding and approach to within a metre of visiting

North Island Robin. Shutterstock/Jo Kleeb

129

South Island Robin. Shutterstock/Ken Griffiths

humans. It's not uncommon for young birds to stand on a person's boot.

Although robins spend a lot of time foraging on the ground, they will also forage over trunks and branches, especially those covered with epiphytes such as mosses. Much of its diet consists of invertebrates but it will also eat small ripe fruit in summer and autumn, when fewer soil-dwelling invertebrates are available. Both species use a variety of strategies to flush out camouflaged prey, such as wing-flicking and tail-flicking.

Occasionally a robin will capture a relatively large prey item which it will kill and dismember, then cache some portions for later retrieval, usually the same or following day. The male and female of a pair will often steal food from each other's hiding places.

Most of the time pairs remain in the same territory, but they may sneak into a neighbouring territory to bathe and drink. Males dominate their mates during the non-breeding season to the extent that pair members are usually found apart. Some birds will change partners between breeding seasons.

Typical nest sites include a tree-fork, or among epiphytes attached to a tree trunk. Only the female incubates and broods the chicks. During this time, the female will call to her mate from the nest every 20 minutes or so to provide her with food. She is particularly susceptible to attack by predators while on the nest. They may take eggs, nestlings and fledglings.

Clutches usually consist of 2–3 eggs. Once the nestlings are more than five days old the male will take the food to the nestling rather than the female. When the nestlings are three weeks old they will leave the nest but continue to be fed by both adults for a further 5–6 weeks.

Pest control operations can help robin populations as well as improving overall forest health. Robust populations of North Island Robins have been established in predator-free fenced sanctuaries or offshore islands. These flourishing populations are used to help repopulate areas where the species may have become locally extinct due to introduced predators.

New Zealand Scaup

Order:	Anseriformes
Family:	Anatidae
Scientific name:	*Aythya novaeseelandiae*
Other names:	black teal, papango, matapouri, titporangi, raipo
New Zealand status:	Endemic
Conservation status:	Not threatened

New Zealand Scaup stamp. New Zealand Post

At 40cm in length, and weighing 695g for a male and 610g for a female, this small round-bodied diving bird is the country's smallest duck. It spends a lot of time under water, where it obtains most of is food, which includes snails, chironomid larvae and caddisfly larvae, and may include plant material.

The New Zealand Scaup is sociable, and especially so in autumn and winter when it can form dense rafts. These are often in association with Australian Coot, Australasian Shoveler and the rare Great Crested Grebe. Large approachable flocks are a feature of the Rotorua and Queenstown lakeshores, while scaup are also commonly seen on the Avon River where it flows through Christchurch.

This species has a fast wing-beat but is a relatively weak flyer and will often fly just above the water. It will sometimes rest on land but usually in a place where it can quickly return to the water if disturbed. Its population is thinly spread on clearwater lakes and lagoons in both the North and South Islands, but is more common on large deep freshwater lakes and hydroelectric lakes. It will often congregate in sheltered areas near willows or reedbeds and will move to more favourable positions as conditions change.

Walter Buller noted: 'It has been seen on mountain lakes. It is becoming increasingly common on shallow lowland lakes, slow-flowing rivers and saltwater.'

New Zealand Scaup tends to be non-migratory and will either nest alone or in a loose colony. Only the females incubate and care for the young, which often form creches, although solitary males or flocks of males have often been seen close to breeding sites.

Breeding occurs mainly between October and March, with the nest well concealed on the ground close to the water. It may be open, partially covered or concealed. The female will often line the nest with down plucked from her own body.

Clutch sizes range from 2–13 eggs, with incubation lasting 29–31 days. When alarmed the chicks will paddle out towards the centre of the lake while the female attempts to distract the source of danger closer to the shore.

New Zealand Scaup.

The species declined following early European settlement due to sport shooting with dogs and habitat destruction, but was given complete protection in 1934 and has since recovered with the 1990s population estimated to be 20,000 birds. Given recent reported sightings it seems likely it has expanded its range with a corresponding increase in population.

Male South Island Tomtit. Shutterstock/Brian Scantlebury

New Zealand Tomtit

Order:	Passeriformes
Family:	Petroicidae
Scientific name:	*Petroica macrocephala*; North Island subspecies *toitoi*, South Island subspecies *macrocephala*
Other names:	[North Island] miromiro, pied tit; [South Island] Ngirungiru, yellow-breasted tit
New Zealand status:	Endemic
Conservation status:	Not threatened

Male North Island Tomtit.
Shutterstock/Martin Pelanek

Both mainland subspecies are common within their ranges on their respective islands. Three other subspecies are restricted to the Chatham Islands, Auckland Islands and Snares Islands and are not covered here.

This small, elegant, active, spritely black-and-white bird adapted well to human arrival and became one of the species most commonly found in settled districts, but due to predation and land clearances its numbers dropped. Today it is well established in exotic pine forests and is commonly found in most native New Zealand forests where there is an abundant native understorey.

Tomtits feed on small insects and their larvae and favour the destructive orchard aphid. They often feed by scanning a wide area then pouncing on prey.

The first sign of the bird's presence is often a repetitive, warbling whistle that normally lasts for 2–3 seconds and is said to resemble the sound of a squeaky wheelbarrow; it is similar to the call of the Grey Warbler but is shorter and not as musical. Males and females have different contact calls – *swee* for the male and *seet* for the female.

The plain white breast of the North Island male differentiates it from its South Island relation, which has an orange and yellow breast. The males of both subspecies are often pugnacious during the breeding season and will often fight for no apparent reason.

Each pair may raise up to three clutches during a breeding season that lasts from September to January, with the female incubating while the male feeds her.

North Island Kokako

Order:	Passeriformes
Family:	Callaeidae
Scientific name:	*Callaeas wilsoni*
Other names:	blue-wattled crow, grey ghost, hakako, honga, pakara
New Zealand status:	Endemic
Conservation status:	Recovering
Other information:	By popular acclaim, the North Island Kokako was voted Bird of the Year in 2016. It appears on the New Zealand $50 bank note.

North Island Kokako. Shutterstock/Frank Booth

This species and the probably extinct South Island Kokako belong to the New Zealand wattlebird family Callaeidae, which also includes the extinct Huia and endangered North Island and South Island Saddlebacks. This handsome bird, with its beautifully soft silky feathers, rakish mask and a long-curved tail, can live up to 24 years and is about the same size of an Australian Magpie. Because of its short rounded wings it can only fly short distances, although it can glide impressively between trees and down gullies. It is seldom seen away from cover but can sometimes be heard crashing around high in the treetops. It is intelligent and can be inquisitive, shy and crafty.

The kokako lives in podocarp forest of kahikatea, totara, matai and miro where it can be found from 30–60m high in the canopy. It likes clematis flowers, puauhmanga, kaiwhirio, kareao, thistle and wild cabbage and its favourite fruit is that of the native fuchsia. It also eats beetles, cicadas, bag moths, sixpenny insects and the fruit and the leaves of many trees. When feeding it uses its extraordinary long legs and toes like a parrot.

It usually only calls at dawn when the bell-like song of a breeding pair can last up to an hour. The song is loud and varied and ranges from loud cackling to full organ song with beautiful notes to a Tui-like soft talking. Some have described its song as a stunning piece of music: slow, haunting, bell-like and clear. Many observers believe it produces the most beautiful song of any New Zealand native bird.

Kokako from different regions in the North Island sing in different ways, and sometimes birds from the same area sing differently to one another. Generally however, birds living in the same area will share the same local 'dialect,' but there can be huge differences in dialects between populations. As the bird sings it uses its body and wings to accentuate the notes. A chick learning to sing is said to sound like a strangled chicken!

Most pairs will attempt to breed in any season, but a bird will only mate with another which understands its song dialect. This presents problems as birds selected for translocation to any particular site must be from the same territory population. The male will carry food to the incubating female, and both adults will feed the chicks. Productivity per pair varies greatly between seasons due to differences in food availability. Early prolonged flowering and fruiting can result in a prolonged breeding season, with up to three broods and increased fledging rates.

Kokako road sign.

In 1986 there were 350 pairs of North Island Kokako and in 1992 the population remained in decline. This was largely due to predation, some of which may have been by Swamp Harrier and the endemic breeding Long-tailed Cuckoo.

Following the introduction and more intensive use of poisons and an array of new traps, kokako numbers began to show an increase. By 2008 there were 770 pairs. After 1080 operations in the Hunua Ranges in the Auckland region in 2018 its numbers have been reported as 'soaring' and the birds can now also be found in the Kaimai-Mamaku Forest Park and have become established in Auckland's Waitakere Ranges.

In 2018 the Te Aroaro o Kahu Restoration Society claimed the New Zealand Biosecurity Community Award for restoring kokako to the Pirongia State Forest Park, not far from the city of Hamilton. This society has been so successful that kokako are no longer considered endangered in this area.

Today the North Island Kokako bird can be found in Puketi Forest, Tronson Kauri Park, Hunua Ranges, Rangitoto Range, Pureora Forest and Otamatuna Forest of Te Urewera National Park. It can also be found in six mainland ecosanctuary reserves and in four predator-free offshore wildlife sanctuaries, of which Kapiti Island is the most important in terms of maintaining a viable population that will help to combat extinction. Little Barrier Island remains a stronghold with some 100 pairs bounding about like squirrels.

Paradise Shelduck

Order:	Anseriformes
Family:	Anatidae
Scientific name:	*Tadorna variegata*
Other names:	putangitangi, parrie
New Zealand status:	Endemic
Conservation status:	Not threatened
Other information:	Of less conservation concern than any other New Zealand endemic species. New Zealand's most widely distributed wildfowl species.

Named In 1773 by Cook as the 'painted duck,' this is New Zealand's only species of shelduck – a worldwide group of large, often terrestrial waterfowl with goose-like features. The female in particular, with her white head, is easy to identify.

Ancient fossils related to this species have been found in lakebed deposits near the Manuherikia River, St Bathans, in Central Otago, and are thought to indicate its Australasian origins. The bird found there was slightly larger than the existing species.

While pairs are usually seen together, they may be challenged by unpaired individuals. When alarmed both are constantly vocal in flight. The male makes a deep *zonk-zonk* while the female gives a shrill *zeek-zeek*, although there can be variations to both calls which are related to maintaining contact with flocking birds and when defending territory.

Pair of Paradise Shelducks. The female is easily identified by the vivid white head.

The population may exceed 700,000 individuals and the birds can be found in pastoral landscapes, on river flats, in mountain areas, at the heads of protected fiords and bays, and around the shorelines of large lakes and hydroelectric dams. They can also be seen on sports fields and on open grassed areas in cities. They favour farm pasture, wetlands, ponds and high-country rivers, and have

Male Paradise Shelduck.

benefitted enormously from the development of pasture lands with their associated drinking ponds for stock. They can also be found in tussock wetlands, in parks and by rivers in some New Zealand towns and cities. This is especially the case during the summer moulting period from December through to March. It was at this time, when the birds are fat and plump, that the early Maori ate them, and also preserved them in their own fat and then sold them to the early European settlers.

Paradise Shelducks reach sexual maturity at two years. Nests are large and substantial and can be found hidden in high grass, in high or hollow trees, or even in burrows in a bank on top of roofs. Usually 8–9 eggs are laid with the female incubating these for 21–22 days. Ducklings can fly at about eight weeks and are cared for by both parents until they can fend for themselves. Many will stay with their parents for up to three months.

While the species was almost exterminated by overhunting in the 19th century, government regulations were introduced and the organisation Fish and Game New Zealand began to manage the population. Prior to each shooting season a survey is taken of shelduck numbers in each Fish and Game region across the country and a daily kill limit set for each area to ensure each population is maintained in a sustainable way.

In 1981 there were an estimated 120,000 birds. In 2011, when the population was estimated to be 600,000–700,000 birds, 200,000 were shot. In 2017 the total population was assessed at 700,000 birds.

While Paradise Shelducks provide some recreational value, large gatherings can do a lot of damage to agricultural crops such as turnips, cereal crops, and peas, with the consumption of four birds being equivalent to one stock unit. The combined guana can also cause significant damage to pasture.

Rifleman

Order:	Passeriformes
Family:	Acanthisittidae
Scientific name:	*Acanthisitta chloris*
Other names:	titiopouanamu, momo-tawi
New Zealand status:	Endemic
Conservation status:	Not threatened

This bird's name stems from the resemblance of the bird's plumage to the green jackets worn by an early colonial New Zealand infantry regiment. Another reason it became known as a Rifleman may be because as it hunts it spirals in flight, as a bullet does from a rifle.

As a member of the Acanthissittidae family of New Zealand wrens it's related to the Rock Wren. At 80mm long and weighing only 6.5g this dainty little fellow is one third the size of a mouse and the same weight as a Grey Warbler, but it gains the title of smallest bird due to its shorter tail and body length. It is widely but sparsely disributed on both main islands but favours high-altitude beech forests and lowland podocarp forests. In particular it likes mature Tawa forest on the North Island and Manuka/Kanuka and Hakea scrub in the South Island. A Rifleman can live for six years but the normal lifespan is two to three years.

This bird was noted during Cook's voyage into Dusky Sound in 1773 and was considered remarkable in its tireless search for food.

When this charming socially monogamous little bird starts to hunt it will never

Rifleman. Shutterstock/Martin Pelanek

Rifleman. Shutterstock/Martin Pelanek

chase insects in the air but will begin at the foot of a selected tree and then work its way up the trunk and along branches by hopping on its relatively large feet supported by fluttering wings as it gleans food from small crevices in the bark, mosses and lichen.

Adults and young keep in contact by a series of short high-pitched cricket-like *zz-itt* or *zee-zee-zee* calls which are difficult for the human ear to detect. Each bird has its own territory and will traverse this every day. Instances have been recorded where it has even remained in a location when the bush around it was being cut down.

Its dome-shaped nests can be found in a crevice under bark, a hole in a tree, the dead fronds of tree fern trunks, and even on the ground under leaf residues or roots. More unusual nest sites have included inside the cavity of a deer skull left hanging in a shed, in a horse skull and even in a pickle bottle with a narrow neck. In every case the nest will often defy observation as the entrance hole is the smallest possible for the parents. Four eggs are laid on a bed of feathers and moss. Both parents feed the chicks. In the event of a second clutch the first brood may help to feed the chicks.

The Rifleman is known to be predated by Moreporks, rats and stoats. In 2018 it was found to be also predated by Long-tailed Cuckoo, which will remove nest material from the nest cavity and take nestlings while one or both parents produce a series of long and agitated calls. The same cuckoo will periodically return to the nest until all the nestlings are taken. Investigations are underway to try and determine whether these cuckoos are brood parasites of Rifleman nests and chicks, and therefore whether they may have an important ecological impact on populations.

Rock Wren

Order:	Passeriformes
Family:	Acanthisittidae
Scientific name:	*Xenicus gilviventris*
Other names:	piwauwau, tuke, South Island wren, matuitui
New Zealand status:	Endemic
Conservation status:	Nationally endangered
Other information:	2012 Bird of the Year

This tiny, reclusive alpine bird – the Edmund Hillary of the bird world – lives in high-altitude boulder fields, scree slopes and cliff systems of cirques and basins in the Southern Alps. Its population is unknown.

This species, together with the Rifleman, belongs to the sister group of all other passerines. As such it is regarded as a living fossil and it is thought to have separated from the now extinct Bush Wren millions of years ago when North and South Islands may have been joined by a land bridge.

The Rock Wren is mainly insectivorous but will also eat berries and seeds, and even sip nectar from flax flowers. In the open they will sometimes flutter up and catch insects on the wing, but primarily they prefer to peck the substrate, grubbing for millipedes, beetles and so forth. They have been observed systematically gleaning through hebe and coprosma bushes, moving through the branches like mice. They also have a habit of calling loudly and bobbing from the top of rocks.

The species is restricted to small pockets of subalpine and alpine habitats along the Southern Alps, from the Murchison Mountains in the south to Kahurangi National Park on the north of the West Coast. It can normally be found from 900m upwards, often to over 2,400m, which is well above the tree line; a few have been found higher.

Rock Wrens make elaborate nests in a rock crevice on the ground, constructed from a dense woven mat shell of tussock stalks, moss, lichen and twigs, and insulated with a thick felting of feathers. One of these nesting crevices held more than 700 Weka feathers, with the rest being from kiwi, Kakapo, Kea and Kereru. As a result, the nests are kept as warm as 30°C to help the birds last out the cold winter. Some scientists believe the bird may have a period of semi-hibernation during the harshest conditions when temperatures drop below freezing. With an entrance the size of a mouse hole, Rock Wren nests are difficult to find.

Walter Buller described: 'trying to acquire a specimen like trying to shoot a mouse'.

The bird's mountainous habitat has protected it from some introduced predators, but nesting on the ground makes it an easy target, particularly for stoats. Climate change is anticipated to affect the species in the future – as the temperature warms its

Rock Wren. Shutterstock/Andrey Chudy

environment will become more suitable for other predators such as rats.

Nesting areas have been monitored for a few years. This has shown that in areas where pest control measures against mustelids and mice have been in place, 85 per cent of Rock Wren nests have been successful. In areas without such protection, the nesting success rate has been 0–30 per cent.

In the 1980s Otago University student Sue Michelsen-Heath was beginning her MSc research project on the breeding biology of the bird in the Mackenzie Basin in the Murchison Mountains, west of Te Anau, and found a Rock Wren nest torn apart by a stoat. She reported that the female kept returning repeatedly to the nest site and pecked among the ruins, searching for her chicks.

Studies following a 1080 poison operation in the Grange area of Kahurangi National Park showed that 85 per cent of Rock Wren nests were successful, compared

Rock Wrens habitually bob and flick their wings. Shutterstock/Agami Photo Agency

to just 30 per cent in nearby areas without pest control. In these non-treated areas up to 33 per cent of females went missing, presumably preyed on by stoats. Other sites without pest control in the Haast Range of South Westland and Lake Roe in Fiordland also showed poor nesting success rates of 17 per cent and 20 per cent respectively.

In 2005 the DOC translocated 28 Rock Wrens to Anchor Island sanctuary in Fiordland, but these failed to establish and disappeared in a few weeks. Attempts at translocations to the Murchison Mountains and to Secretary Island sanctuary have been more encouraging.

In 2007–08 snowstorms repeatedly lashed the Murchison, after which 248 man-hours were spent searching the Mackenzie basin to only find 34 pairs, of which 14 were observed to produce fledgings. This study revealed that the bird's range had decreased by a quarter compared to what it had been in 1984, thus suggesting a downward trend in the population of the species.

Saddlebacks

	North Island Saddleback	South Island Saddleback
Order:	Passeriformes	Passeriformes
Family:	Callaeidae	Callaeidae
Scientific name:	*Philesturnus rufuster*	*Philesturnus carunculatus*
Other names:	tieke	tieke
New Zealand status:	Endemic	Endemic
Conservation status:	Recovering	Recovering

Prior to the forest clearances of the 1800s and the introduction of predators, saddlebacks were widespread throughout both the North and South Islands. Both species are about 25cm long, weigh about 80g, and have a distinctive chestnut saddle which develops before the birds leave the nest. The male of the North Island species has a narrow yellowish line along the upper edge of the saddle which is lacking in the South Island bird.

Saddlebacks are members of the family of New Zealand wattlebirds that also includes Huia, Stitchbird and kokako. Male saddlebacks have larger wattles than females. In both cases these are not fully developed until 6–8 months old but continue to grow in size and coloration until the bird reaches adulthood.

These birds are fearless, cheeky, inquisitive and very vocal. The typical call is a *chee-per-per-chee-per-par* repeated in quick succession. The males have a repertoire of melodic calls for use during mating and territorial disputes. Phrases of some vocalisations are often shared between neighbours and are important in maintaining territories year-round.

Male North Island Saddleback.
Shutterstock/Martin Pelanek

Male South Island Saddleback.
Shutterstock/Agami Photo Agency

Saddlebacks are often found on the ground in coastal forests, probing through dead wood and leaf litter for weta, grubs and other insects with their strong bills. They also eat the fruit of forest trees such a kawaka and coprosma and will take nectar. They are such vigorous feeders that sometimes New Zealand Fantails and Whiteheads will accompany them, hovering to catch any dislodged insects.

Saddlebacks will normally nest in a cavity of some sort and will use the same nest year after year, making any necessary repairs before producing a clutch of three eggs.

Maori found it hard to snare these birds for food, but when they caught one it was usually kept and tethered so that it would give warning of enemy approaching, hence its Maori name of Tieke which means guardian.

The South Island Saddleback was saved from extinction in 1964 when 36 birds were translocated from rat-infested Big South Cape Island (off Stewart Island) to nearby Big and Kaimohu Islands. This was the first time that any such rescue translocation had been attempted anywhere in the world. More than 30 descendants from this translocation have been introduced or reintroduced to other predator-free mainland sites, including Bushy Park Tarapuruhi and Orokonui Ecosanctuary near Dunedin, and to offshore islands.

Due to its tendency to forage, roost and nest low to the ground the South Island Saddleback remains extremely vulnerable to predation by rats and stoats. In 1971 the International Union for the Conservation of Nature Red Data Book devoted a single full page to this bird. At the end of this page, it read: 'Those New Zealand ornithologists who planned and executed the remarkable rescue of this species indeed deserve the congratulations of all conservationists.'

The only remaining small natural population of North Island Saddleback is on the offshore Taranga (Hen) Island. Like its South Island relative, the North Island Saddleback was confined to predator-free offshore islands until Zealandia Ecosanctuary in Wellington received the first translocation to a mainland sanctuary site in 2002.

In subsequent years pairs were found breeding at nearby Birdwood Reserve, Wrights Hill and Polhill Reserve. It's been estimated that the area could support a population of 300 birds. In May 2017 Wellington City Council established a programme to band these birds in the hope of learning more about those that venture outside the fenced safety of Zealandia. Many well-organised volunteers are carrying out intensive pest-trapping and monitoring programmes. All these activities are, in part, being funded by WWF New Zealand and Predator Free New Zealand.

Elsewhere the North Island Saddleback was reintroduced to the mainland at Taranaki on 10 May 2014 after an absence of 150 years; it was introduced to Rotokare Scenic Reserve and pest-free sanctuary after a 395km trip by helicopter and car from Little Barrier Island north of Auckland.

Shore Plover

Order:	Charadriiformes
Family:	Charadriidae
Scientific name:	*Thinornis novaeseelandiae*
Other names:	shore dotterel, tuturuatu, sand plover, New Zealand plover, New Zealand shore plover
New Zealand status:	Endemic
Conservation status:	Nationally Critical

Shore Plover. Shutterstock/Agami Photo Agency

This stocky and colourful little bird is one of the world's rarest shorebird species; possibly as few as 150 remain. It was once found around the New Zealand coast but became extinct on the North and South Islands by the 1870s, leaving the Chatham Islands as its last outpost.

The Shore Plover breeds in monogamous pairs and will vigorously defend its territory. It almost always nests under vegetation, boulders or driftwood, laying eggs from October. Incubation takes about 28 days and is shared by both parents, with the male usually taking the night shift. If a clutch is lost they will continue laying replacement clutches until January.

Pairs keep in contact with soft *chip* calls while the territorial call is a loud, rapid ringing, somewhat like a young oystercatcher piping.

These birds are strong flyers and juveniles disperse widely, although they will usually return to their natal site to breed. Several birds have returned from release sites to the captive-breeding institutions where they were reared. Some of these flights were over 380km, while one bird flew 850km in two months.

In 2019 more than 20 chicks were hatched from seven captive-breeding pairs at Pukaha National Wildlife Centre, Mount Bruce. This was the most successful season since the Shore Plover Recovery Programme began in the 1980s, and represented an almost a 10 per cent increase in the total population of 250 birds. About 500 of the captive-bred birds have been released on predator-free islands off the New Zealand mainland, but with mixed success; a small population seems to be persisting on Motutapu island in the Hauraki Gulf, with some birds being seen in the wider Auckland area in 2019, raising hopes for its future prospects.

As the species is particularly vulnerable to predator incursions, intensive predator management has gradually reduced the risk of extinction, but by early 2016 the total wild population was only 175 adults. Shore Plovers are now managed at mainland captive-breeding sites such as the Pukaha National Wildlife Centre, Isaac Wildlife and Conservation Trust, Peacock Springs and Motutapu Island. In addition to mammalian predation, the species is also susceptible to predation by Black-billed Gull, Swamp Harrier and Morepork.

South Island Pied Oystercatcher

Order:	Charadriiformes
Family:	Haematopodidae
Scientific name:	*Haematopus finschi*
Other names:	SIPO, Finsch's oystercatcher, torea, New Zealand pied oystercatcher
New Zealand status:	Endemic
Conservation status:	Declining

South Island Pied Oystercatcher. Shutterstock/Imogen Warren

Oystercatchers are a widespread group containing a single genus, *Haematopus*. They were hunted for sport until 1940. With a population of about 112,000 birds in 1994, the South Island Pied Oystercatcher remains the most common oystercatcher species in New Zealand.

At 46cm and weighing 550g it is solidly built and a strong flyer. It also has highly ritualised displays. During breeding it will use loud piping displays to warn off other oystercatchers and other intruders.

It is found on most estuaries across the country in good numbers, with most being seen in December–July. Its main North Island feeding grounds include the Firth of Thames near Auckland city, Farewell Spit at the top of the South Island, and the Kaipara and Manukau harbours.

In August most of the adult population will fly to the South Island to breed, on inland riverbeds east of the Southern Alps, high-country grassland or farmland. Many will also breed on coastal lagoons and estuaries.

After raising young, in December the birds return to their coastal feeding grounds in the North and South Islands, where large flocks gather at sand spits, estuaries and river mouths. They probe into mud or wet sand for mussels, oysters, limpets and crabs, and will also pick from the surface. After heavy rain they often move to farmland to feed on worms and insect larvae.

Pair bonds are not maintained outside the breeding season, but most birds retain their partner from one breeding season to the next. Banding shows that about 89 per cent of adults survive from one season to the next and it is believed that the oldest birds could live for about 25 years.

The nest is an unlined scrape on a mound or raised area of gravel, sand or soil, above spring-tide level and offering good all-round visibility. The female and male take turns incubating the 1–3 eggs for 24–28 days. The young can fly six weeks after hatching.

Spotted Shag

Order:	Suliformes
Family:	Phalacrocoracidae
Scientific name:	*Phalacrocorax punctatus*
Other names:	kawau, tikitiki, parekareka, spotted cormorant, blue shag (southern form), *Stictocarbo punctatus*
New Zealand status:	Endemic
Conservation status:	Not threatened

Spotted Shag.

New Zealand is at the global epicentre of biodiversity for the shag and cormorant family. Of the world's 40 or so species 12 occur on New Zealand's main islands and its island groups, and eight of these species are endemic. They are the country's only cliff-nesting birds. The Spotted Shag is the most common and widespread of the endemic species. One writer eloquently described this elegant bird as being: 'Like a city gentleman in a suit.'

In summer the Spotted Shag population is concentrated around its stronghold breeding sites in the Marlborough Sounds, Banks Peninsula and on the Otago Coast. It is never found inland, favouring coastal inlets, estuaries and harbours to feed and roost. These birds feed in deep water up to 15km from shore, where its longest recorded dive was for 70 seconds. The oldest recorded Spotted Shag was 10 years.

Colonies range in size from a few pairs to a few hundred pairs. The birds are monogamous and the timing of breeding varies from colony to colony as food becomes available. Clutches of 3–4 eggs are laid in large nests made of sticks, iceplant and grass, which are positioned 1m apart on coastal cliffs and on rock stacks. Incubation and chick-rearing is shared by the parents and the chicks are continuously guarded. The young leave the nest at 62 days.

When at rest, nesting and roosting, the Spotted Shag calls with loud grunts; elsewhere it remains silent. Outside the breeding season it forms large feeding and roosting flocks of up to 2,000 birds.

Normally adults remain within 200km of their nesting grounds year-round, although some may travel up to 300km, while juveniles can wander more widely. This species' habit of nesting in sites that are difficult to survey, and often changing nesting sites, makes population trends hard to assess, although at present it is estimated that up to 30,000 pairs breed across New Zealand.

Today the Spotted Shag is commonly found around the coasts of South Island and off the coast of Wellington. In the early 1900s a Spotted Shag population numbering in the thousands existed in the Hauraki Gulf region near Auckland, breeding on the inner gulf islands along the sides of the Coromandel Peninsula and roosting on the Firth of Thames. It also once bred on the west coast of Waikato. By the 1930s this population had crashed to just a few hundred birds.

It is known that the early Hauraki Gulf population fed on an abundance of pilchards and anchovies and the near-demise of the bird is likely related to the close-extinction of these food sources. It is also thought that this loss of a food source resulted in the birds slowly changing their foraging habits and diet, switching to small fish and marine vertebrates including squid and plankton. This hypothesis is supported by the fact that the carbon isotope signature of the present populations is less enriched than in birds from the 1880s (which were assessed using museum specimens).

Mitochondrial and nuclear DNA have shown that, contrary to popular belief,

Spotted Shag.

Spotted Shags from northern New Zealand form a geographically restricted haplogroup which is distinct from the southern populations.

Spotted Shags often have a mass of small stones in the gizzard, which roosting birds regurgitate. The function of these is not yet fully understood but the possibilities include a role as ballast, for grinding up food, or for creating an inhospitable environment for gut parasites.

Stitchbird

Order:	Passeriformes
Family:	Notiomystidae
Scientific name:	*Notiomystis cincta*
Other names:	hihi
New Zealand status:	Endemic
Conservation status:	Nationally vulnerable

One of New Zealand's rarer birds, the Stitchbird is a relative of the saddlebacks, although their evolutionary lines diverged as far back as 39 million years ago. The male is 18cm in length and weighs 36.4g while the female is smaller and lighter at 30g. Like many of New Zealand's endemic birds, the Stitchbird did not cope well

Male Stitchbird. Shutterstock/Imogen Warren

with the changes to its habitat and environment wrought by humans and the pest species they brought with them.

Until 2006 the Stitchbird was classified as belonging to honeyeater family Meliphagidae, which includes the Bellbird and Tui. However, genetic studies suggested that it should be placed in a family of its own, the Notiomystidae, and that its closest relatives are the Huia, kokako and saddlebacks in the New Zealand wattlebird family Callaeidae.

The Stitchbird is essentially a forest dweller with a diet consisting of nectar, berries and insects. Breeding takes place in November–December when a clutch of up to five eggs is laid. The presence of Stitchbirds can be an indicator of forest health and a test of ecological restoration. For these reasons it symbolises life, vigour, and the good health of the forest.

Its habit of nesting in tree holes and cavities 3–13m above the ground makes

Female Stitchbird. Shutterstock/Imogen Warren

it particularly vulnerable to predation by rats, stoats and cats. It's also believed that diseases carried by introduced exotic bird species may have contributed to the Stitchbird's decline.

The sexes are easy to tell apart as the female looks quite different to the male and has more subdued colouring. The call is a distinct *titch*, but it also has a collection of whistles, warbles and a penetrating alarm call described as *yeng yeng yeng*. Males also have a distinctive *see-si-ip* call.

Stitchbirds have a fascinating and complex mating system. A male will pair up with a female in its territory while also seeking to mate with other females in the neighbourhood. To ensure the chicks are his, the male has to produce a large amount of sperm to dilute that of other males. To avoid wasting his time he also needs to be able to quickly assess exactly when a female is ready to breed. In the days leading up to laying, when the female is laden with eggs, some males may chase her for hours at a time, all attempting to mate with her. In addition, the Stitchbird is the only bird species known to occasionally mate face to face.

Prior to European arrival the Stitchbird was common enough in the North Island for Maori to take it for food and feathers for making ceremonial cloaks, but the last recorded sighting was in the Tararua Ranges in 1883. It was declared extinct on the North Island mainland in 1885, with only a tiny remnant population existing on Little Barrier Island in the Hauraki Gulf. In 1918 it was thought that the South Island population was unlikely to exceed 2,000 birds.

Since the 1980s translocated birds have been established on a number of predator-free offshore islands.

In 2005 the Zealandia Ecosanctuary made history by becoming the first mainland site on North Island to host the species in 120 years, using birds from South Island. Following the development of successful translocation strategies, small populations now also exist in the other mainland sanctuaries such as Bushy Park and Rotokare near Stratford, and in the Mountain Maungatautari Sanctuary, which has the longest predator-proof fence in the world.

In every case artificial nest boxes and supplementary feeding are provided. Breeding activity is closely monitored by removing infertile eggs to encourage subsequent breeding attempts, and cross-fostering where needed. Nest boxes are also sprayed to prevent mite infestations which can kill young chicks.

In 2019 the Hihi Conservation Charitable Trust reported that 252 new birds were produced on Tiritiri Matangi island, making this the best breeding season ever at the site and a fantastic result for this nationally vulnerable endemic bird.

South Island Takahe

Order:	Gruiformes
Family:	Rallidae
Scientific name:	*Porphyrio hochstetteri*
Other names:	takahe, notornis
New Zealand status:	Endemic
Conservation status:	Nationally vulnerable

This colourful bird is perhaps the only one to have been considered extinct twice and rediscovered twice. It is believed to have derived from a Pukeko-like ancestor arriving in New Zealand in the Pliocene period, 5.3 million to 2.6 million years ago.

The North Island Takahe and South Island Takahe were considered to be the same species for 147 years until morphometric analyses of the bones of the bird found by Walter Mantell in the North Island and those later examined from South Island birds were found to be different. The North Island bird was found to be closer to the native Pukeko, thus in 1996 the South Island species was recognised and described as South Island Takahe and the North Island species as North Island Takahe or Moho.

South Island Takahe.

Takahe. DOC

South Island Takahe has blue-green plumage and a vivid red bill, and at 63cm in length it is the world's largest rail species. In summer it feeds on grass and the protein-rich leaf bases of three species of mountain tussock and one species of mountain daisy. In winter it retreats to the forest where it digs up ferns and feeds on the rhizomes for up to 19 hours every day. This process is essential in order to obtain the carbohydrates and certain minerals it needs to survive the subzero winter temperatures in its alpine habitat.

In 1849 sealers found large footprints of a bird in the snow-blanketed precipitous landscape bordering the frigid waters of Dusky Sound. These were larger than those of a kiwi. The sealers' dog gave chase and soon caught the bird in an area on the shores of the sound behind Resolution Island. It never tried to fly away but ran quickly and when caught cried loudly and struggled hard.

Walter Mantell was able to obtain its skin. After completing careful drawings of a leg and the head he packed up the skin with his drawings and sent them to his father, Dr Gideon Mantell, who sold them to the British Museum for 25 pounds, but this was only after he paid for the stuffing and mounting himself. The bird remained on

Pukeko or Australasian Swamphen, *Porphyrio porphyrio.*

Adult South Island Takahe feeding a young bird. Shutterstock/Anna Dunlop

display in the museum alongside the extinct Dodo of Mauritius until it was returned to New Zealand in 1953.

Another takahe was found on the eastern side of Lake Te Anau in 1879, while in 1898 the rabbiter Bob Scott found a third when one of his dogs brought it to him in its mouth. This one was purchased by the Otago Museum for 150 pounds, which was a princely sum in those days. The same year Jack Ross and his dog caught a fourth specimen, again on the shores of Lake Te Anau.

History suggests Maori once hunted takahe near Te Anau and made an annual excursion to do so. A Ms Cameron of Centre Island in Lake Te Anau stated that two specimens were killed and eaten by Maori in 1878, who described them to her as resembling Pukeko but the size of a turkey. There was once an ancient Maori village near the present Te Anau township and a smaller village about 2km west of Te Anau, but by 1848 these had been abandoned.

In 1919 young Geoffrey Orbell visited the Otago Museum with his father and became fascinated by the mounted takahe he saw. By 1929 he was a medical specialist, a keen deerstalker and had built a family crib (home) on the shore of the small township of Te Anau. This overlooked the lake and the Murchison Mountains beyond.

During his deerstalking forays into the Fiordland wilderness he kept looking for signs of the takahe and eventually developed a theory that they might be found in the high alpine valleys above the bush line. On 11 April 1943 he was deerstalking

Takahe. Shutterstock/Hugh Lansdown

with two others in the Murchison Mountains when he saw some unusual footprints, the big toes bent inwards just like the bird in the Otago Museum. He also found chewed tussock. Although convinced he had rediscovered sound evidence of the bird's presence, he failed to convince Robert Falla, the director of the Canterbury Museum.

Not to be deterred, he continued his quest and eventually sighted two birds. Knowing that the bird was considered to have been extinct for 50 years, and bruised by his encounter with Robert Falla, he decided not to say a word until he had rock-solid evidence, and in 1945 he renewed his search.

In July 1947 Alice McKenzie saw what she thought was a takahe on her family run in the Hollyford Valley of Fiordland. But when she later saw the specimen in the Otago museum, she thought the bird she had seen was shorter than that and had different coloured legs. In the 23 years until the run was sold no one claimed to have seen another one.

Finally, on 20 November 1948 Dr Orbell returned to the site in the Murchison Mountains where he had first seen the birds. Taking his movie camera and accompanied by Rex Watson and Neil McCrosbie he photographed two takahe in colour. At one point he said to his friends: 'It's either a Pukeko or isn't.' This event took place exactly 100 years after Professor Owen of the British Museum had named the first takahe. Fittingly, a year later he introduced Robert Falla to the species in what by then had become known as Takahe Valley. To mark this occasion the Ornithological Society of New Zealand renamed its journal *Notornis*.

Takahe can live for up to 25 years and begin breeding at three years of age. The female incubates the eggs during the day and the male at night. The species forms strong family groupings. Often a one-year-old juvenile will stay with its parents and help raise a new chick as, usually, only one chick will be strong enough to look after itself. Adult pairs are always 'talking' to each other by making constant clucking sounds rather like a hen, and they continue doing this even when out of visual contact.

The birds are very territorial and will fight to defend their patch using their strong legs and bill. In the process they can bite, hold on to, kick and pull out feathers from an opponent.

Initially it was thought the safest thing to do with the newly found population was to leave the birds alone in their natural habitat and declare the rugged Murchison Mountains a special area which was off limits to all but scientists and deer hunters.

However, in 1957 a captive-breeding programme was established in a safe and secure area at Pukaha Mount Bruce National Wildlife Centre in the Wairarapa, where conditions are wet but not as extreme as in Fiordland. Unfortunately, these birds spent their time engaged in territorial disputes rather than mating. This issue was resolved by creating small neutral zones between the pens and providing nutrients in the birds' drinking water. Fertility increased and the first chick was successfully reared.

In 1972 the Wildlife Service found only a few birds in the Murchison Mountains when it had been assumed that there were hundreds. Some of these were 20km from Takahe Valley. This situation was attributed to a deterioration in the quality of tussock

The day of discovery. Allied Press

Robert Falla (left) in Takahe Valley
with Geoffrey Orbell. Allied Press

Feeding young takahe using gloved imitations.

Takahe survey party in the Murchison Mountains. DOC

due to a sudden influx of red deer combined with predation by stoats.

As a result of culling deer the population of birds in the wild increased to nearly 200 but it was later found that during 'mega mast' years for beech trees the Murchisons were besieged by plagues of stoats which could halve the takahe population within months. Fortunately by this stage many captive-reared takahe had been established in various mainland and island sanctuaries.

In response an existing stoat-trapping programme has been expanded to cover the whole 50,000 hectares of the Murchison Mountains. Testing and refining the effectiveness of stoat and deer control programmes is now at the centre of work there, with about one third of the adult population of takahe fitted with transmitters. This allows regular monitoring of the remaining takahe in the wild, so as to ascertain rates of survival and causes of death. Data collected shows that the Murchison Mountains population declines naturally and requires supplementation with captive-bred birds in order to maintain it.

The initial 20 years of attempts at captive-breeding programmes only achieved limited success, with four chicks from 70 eggs reared to independence. By the early 1980s there were only 118 takahe in existence, so in 1985 a purpose-built captive-breeding facility was established at Burwood Bush near Te Anau, where the lessons learned from previous failures and successes were applied. Eggs were taken from the wild and were flown to Burwood, where they were incubated and reared using glove puppets that imitated adult takahe in order to brood and feed them and thus minimise human contact.

After seven weeks the chicks were released into a 3,000-hectare enclosure of red tussock and beech forest. Having no human contact they adapted quickly, and the number of young successfully reared there increased the population numbers much faster than the birds could in the wild.

Initially the Burwood birds were not returned to the Murchisons, but used to establish other wild populations in other suitable areas as an insurance policy.

Today, all Burwood birds are returned to the Murchisons. Further, because puppet-reared takahe were shown to have a lower productivity than naturally reared birds, this prompted a shift away from expensive artificial rearing and allowed a greater number of breeding pairs to hatch and raise chicks themselves. In the process great care is taken to maintain genetic diversity.

Management practices have continued to evolve. The centre now keeps up to 25 pairs of takahe in 1-hectare natural tussock pens within a 135-hectare grass/beech forest enclosure where the birds are left to incubate the eggs on their nests and rear the chicks themselves. Rangers intervene as necessary using nest-manipulation techniques whereby infertile eggs are removed to encourage the birds to lay again, or the infertile eggs are replaced with fertile ones from another nest.

The long-term goal is to return takahe to the areas where they once lived and create self-sustaining populations with high levels of genetic diversity and equal sex ratios to maximise breeding potential. The focus on creating new wild populations in areas where the species once lived appears to be proving successful. By 2019 there were 10 such sanctuaries with a total breeding population of 100 pairs and a total population of 347 birds. For example, in 2018 a new wild population was established in the Gouland Downs of the Kahurangi National Park; in its first year this new population produced at least two chicks.

Takahe statue in Te Anau. Shutterstock/Robert CHG

Tui

Order:	Passeriformes
Family:	Meliphagidae
Scientific name:	*Prosthemadera novaeseelandiae*
Other names:	parson bird, koko, tute, tuuii, mockingbird
New Zealand status:	Endemic
Conservation status:	Not threatened
Other information:	New Zealand Bird of the Year 2005

Old Tui stamp.
New Zealand Post

This treasured iconic bird is well known throughout the country and only absent from dry country and the Southern Alps. It is also one of the few endemic bird species to have survived and thrived in the presence of humans and to have adapted to the many changes they wrought. Like the kiwi it has entered our national conscience like no other bird. Many people plant flax, kowhai, puriri and Australian flowering shrubs to attract this nectar-loving bird into their gardens.

It is one of the most widely and commonly illustrated bird species in New Zealand and its image has appeared on the New Zealand 1936 penny stamp, the one shilling stamp and on many subsequent stamp issues.

For many people the Tui is common enough to be a familiar sight. Real estate agents frequently allude to resident Tui as a selling point of houses. Visitors to New Zealand Parliament in Wellington are likely to see the bird enjoying the Pohutukawa flowers there. It even has a brewery carrying its name.

In his second voyage to Dusky Sound, Cook wrote of the Tui: 'Under its throat hang two little tufts of snow-white feathers, called poes, which is the Otaheitean word for 'earrings' and occasioned us giving that name to the bird, which is not more remarkable for its beauty of a plumage than the sweetness of its notes. The flesh is also most delicious and the greatest luxury the wood afforded us.'

Joseph Banks agreed, noting: 'Its plumage, like its singing and the tastiness of its flesh, was treasured by Maori when it was fat with berries in the late autumn and other food was scarce.' He also reported: 'Its beautiful feathers were a prized component for woven cloaks.'

The Tui is a noisy and usually solitary bird that is normally seen in the treetops, where it can often be heard chortling and chuckling. Sometimes birds can catch the unwary by whizzing past at a disconcerting waist- or shoulder-height.

As the dominant New Zealand honeyeater species it is courageous, aggressive and pugnacious and will chase other birds, especially Kereru, other Tui and Bellbirds, from its feeding territory. It has also been known to attack Swamp Harriers and Australian

Tui.

Magpies, but will feed with other birds on a tree outside its territory. It will also eat fruit and large insects. Importantly, it is one of the more common pollinators of flowering plants and plays a role in forest regeneration as it can disperse the seeds of medium-sized fruits.

Some Tui have been seen to jump around and beat a bush in order to disturb stick insects and cicadas. Both sexes have notched wing-tips but those of the male are larger. These allow it to beat the air heavily, thereby announcing itself as a heavy weight and achieving control of food.

Its loud rasping song is familiar to most New Zealanders and for many people it's the equivalent to the nightingale among New Zealand's birds, for it has a wide variety of calls that combine Bellbird-like notes with clicks, cackles, groans and wheezes. Its contact call is a melodious *hiccup*, but it can burst into marvellous song. As it possesses a dual voice box, it is famed for its mimicry and is thought to have hundreds of sounds at its disposal. It can exactly recreate sounds such as telephone rings, glass shattering, car alarms, beeps, whistles and other sounds. It can also remember some words and short sentences. Some of its sounds can be too high for the human ear to hear, so if an apparently silent bird is seen with its beak open and chest puffed out it may be singing.

A Tui nest is an untidy structure of large twigs and roots lined with finer twigs, lichen, tree fern scales and moss. The birds site this in dense vegetation, in a forked branch or against a tree trunk. A clutch of 2–4 eggs is laid between September and November and the chicks fledge at 11–20 days and are independent after two weeks.

Outside the breeding season Tui may become partially nomadic and travel from breeding territories to towns, rural gardens and forest patches in search of nectar and fruit. These feeding territories can be more than 20km apart and the birds will fly up to 10km a day to seek nectar.

Early Maori often kept Tui in cages, trained them to speak and even used them to welcome visitors to a marae. On occasions the brushed ends of the tongue would be trimmed so that a bird could speak more clearly. Many of these birds became famous and were even fought over. Maori also trapped them and potted them in calabashes to preserve the meat so that it could be eaten at special feasts.

Variable Oystercatcher

Order:	Charadriiformes
Family:	Haematopodidae
Scientific name:	*Haematopus unicolor*
Other names:	black oystercatcher, torea tai, torea pango, torea
New Zealand status:	Endemic
Conservation status:	Recovering

This species has different colour morphs. Some are black all over, some have a smudged black-and-white belly, and some have a pure white belly. These morphs interbreed freely and belong to a single species.

Measuring 48cm and weighing 725g the Variable Oystercatcher it is larger, more heavily built and more robust than the South Island Pied Oystercatcher, but with a population of only about 5,000 birds it is rarer than that species. Previously it was shot for food, although it has been protected since 1907.

The Variable Oystercatcher is a familiar sight on rocky and sandy beaches,

Pied-morph Variable Oystercatcher.

Dark-morph Variable Oystercatcher. Shutterstock/Imogen Warren

sand dunes, sandspits and estuaries around the coast of Northland, Auckland, the Coromandel, Bay of Plenty, Greater Wellington, Nelson/Marlborough and Fiordland. It can often be seen probing for invertebrates, molluscs and crustaceans, and also foraging in nearby paddocks.

In the mid-1990s the population was about 4,000 birds. By 2013 this is thought to have increased to 5,000 or 6,000 birds, but this increase may slow as the species' feeding areas reach capacity.

The birds are very vocal and use loud piping calls in territorial interactions and when alarmed. They will also use a loud flight call that is very similar to that of other oystercatchers. Adults warn chicks of danger with a sharp, loud *chip* or *click*.

Variable Oystercatchers are monogamous, with adults showing high fidelity to their mate and their nesting site. They will defend a territory vigorously against neighbours and also people who venture close to the nest, eggs and chicks. They can breed from 2 years old and live for at least 30 years.

The nest is usually a simple scape in the sand. Eggs are laid from September to October and replaced if lost. Chicks can fly at 6–7 weeks and are defended by both parents. Due to disturbance from human recreational use of the coast, losses from mammalian and avian predators, and the flooding of nest sites by high tides, rates of breeding can be slow.

Weka

Order:	Gruiformes
Family:	Rallidae
Scientific name:	*Gallirallus australis*
Other names:	Maori hen, woodhen
New Zealand status:	Endemic
Conservation status:	There are four weakly differentiated subspecies: North Island (at risk/recovering); Buff (at risk); Western (not threatened); and Stewart Island (threatened/nationally vulnerable)

At 50cm long this flightless member of the rail family grows to the size of a hen. While primarily carnivorous it's also omnivorous so will eat invertebrates, fruit, eggs, grubs, snails, mice, carrion, grain crops and in fact almost anything. It can easily kill small animals such Norway rats and birds up to the size of the Westland Petrel. It's a good swimmer and was once commonly found over large areas of both the North and South Islands from sea level to above the snowline.

Although it can fly it prefers to run, using its wings to assist with balance. It has remarkably good eyesight, is far from cowardly, is well able to defend itself and when pressed will fight to the death.

It was an important food source for early Maori who respected its intelligence and resilience: 'When a Weka breaks from a snare, it won't be back.'

Captain Cook reported: 'As they cannot fly, they inhabit the skirts of the woods, and feed on sea-beach and are so tame, or foolish, as to stare at us till we knock them down with a stick.' He also noted that: 'They eat well in a pie or fricassee.'

Explorer Charlie Douglas was an avid admirer of the 'Maori hen.' He liked its personal valour, its undying thirst for knowledge and its intelligence, which he considered far higher than any other bird he had seen. For many other early explorers such as James Hector it was a staple part of their diet.

In 1863 Walter Buller believed that the species was doomed to extinction through starvation. Despite his assessment, and the efforts of mustelids, it made an amazing recovery. But despite years of population growth, populations are prone to sudden declines, and the reasons for this are not fully understood. Buller also noted: 'It has an inordinately voracious appetite and will eat almost anything including fish, shellfish, small rats and kelp.' He reported that one bird ate nearly a hundredweight (50kg) of potatoes in two months.

It has a highly adapted ability to populate habitats in a wide range of environmental conditions from sea level up to 300m provided there is water and cover. These include marginal bush, open scrubland, beaches, semi-open or open farmland

Weka.

and other cultivated areas. Weka particularly like the presence of under-runners, where they can hide in tunnels formed by subsidence in the soil or under sedge which covers walkways. For the same reason they also favour dense cover such as blackberry, inkweed and tall grass crops.

As it has no crop its gizzard contents can provide material for studies to assess its impact on agriculture and home gardens. Studies suggest that the food intake is comparable to that of pheasants, starlings and blackbirds. Like Kea, the Weka is inquisitive, delightful and the most cunning of thieves. Many say it possesses a criminal character. It has an insatiable appetite for collecting and hiding anything left lying about. Its approach to stealing is slow, deliberate, and calculated. The range of items it is known to have stolen is impressive and ranges through potato chips, underwear, a plastic bag containing pyjamas, watches, a wedding ring, razors, a pillow, spoons, a T-shirt, and in fact anything left lying about. One unhappy bushman left his false teeth on a stump by a creek while he had a wash and never saw them again.

Weka possess an extraordinary homing instinct and are capable of swimming up to a kilometre. In one notable case a banded bird removed from Maud Island in the Marlborough Sounds and released several kilometres away on the mainland was back on the island in a few days after a long hike and a 900m swim against the current.

Birds normally call at dawn and dusk with a *coo-et* which is like that of a male kiwi but less harsh and repeated more often. The male's call is louder than the female's. It will also boom, and pairs often use a soft clucking contact call.

Weka mate for life and nest on the ground, in thick bushes or under logs, between August and January. They produce up to three eggs per clutch and can have up to four clutches per year. The chicks are fed by both parents, who will fiercely fight off any predator until the chicks are fully grown.

This species presents a conservation conundrum. As it is known to kill rats and mice and disperse fruit such as that of the hinau tree, all of which makes it a conservation ally, but it also preys on ground-burrowing seabirds, ground-nesting birds and reptiles, making it an enemy. As such it has had to be removed from a few important ecosanctuaries where it was once common.

A chance encounter with a Weka is often a highlight for a tourist who will mistake it for a kiwi. Even when they see that the bird is trying to drag a boot out of a tent, or running in the distance, they invariably still seem to think that it's a kiwi. Some local folk mischievously encourage this by saying: 'It's a southern short-beaked kiwi.'

The bird is rightly celebrated by many people and is the subject of a poem *The Weka* by the famous New Zealand poet Eileen Duggan (1894–1972):

Weka, O weka, O little brown weka,
Why do they hate you, and cry on your name?
They tell me you're sly and swoop without warning,
Your wings have no flight, and your beak, has no shame.
You're gay as a gossip and vain as a man-child,
you snatch at a bright thing and bear it away.
You sing with your mate when all good birds are silent,
You're gallant by night and you're sidelong by day.
But it's my pity your footprints grow rarer,
Little brown mischief, don't slip from our sight,
Wicked and sweet are your eyes in the twilight,
Wistful and wild is your cry in the night.

Wrybill

Order:	Charadriiformes
Family:	Charadriidae
Scientific name:	*Anarhynchus frontalis*
Other names:	pare, ngutua, ngutuparoro
New Zealand status:	Endemic
Conservation status:	Nationally vulnerable
Other information:	Walter Buller called this bird crook-bill plover

In 1869 it was agreed that the Wrybill is the only bird in the world to have a laterally curved bill. It is believed that it uses this as a tool to flip over stones as it seeks mayfly larvae and spiders; it may also be because the bird uses its right eye for close range foraging and the other to better spot predators. In addition, the unique shape forms an open scoop ideal for feeding in mud, while this special adaptation minimises competition for food with other bird species.

There are about 3,500–4,000 individuals of this extremely confiding 20cm bird remaining. From December to early February they breed on the beds of braided rivers close to Southern Alps, where their superb camouflage allows them to blend in perfectly as a protection against aerial predators.

After breeding the majority of Wrybills will normally make a six- or seven-hour flight north to the tidal estuaries and harbours in the North Island, such as the Firth of Thames, before returning south again in early August. These large flocks, a single one of which may contain up to 75 per cent of the entire Wrybill population, have been described as being like a scarf flying in the air.

Each pair will defend their territory and nest alone. The chicks are active after hatching and will follow their parents as they forage for food. Within hours they can swim and, if necessary, hunt for food. The pair will nest again if eggs, chicks or the nest itself are lost due to predators or flood events.

Since 2014 the Wrybill population has been in steady decline with an annual rate of loss of about 10 per cent. The full cause or causes of this is not yet fully understood.

Wrybill in breeding plumage showing its unique bill. Shutterstock/Imogen Warren

Feeding Wrybill. Shutterstock/Imogen Warren

Whitehead

Order:	Passeriformes
Family:	Pachycephalidae
Scientific name:	*Mohoua albicilla*
Other names:	popokotea, bush canary
New Zealand status:	Endemic
Conservation status:	Declining

This gregarious little songbird is only found in the North Island, where it lives in noisy groups of up to eight family members. While it favours the canopy of tall dense native forests and scrubland, it can also be found in mature pine plantations. In all habitats it is usually more often heard than seen. The song is a characteristic *viu viu viu zir zir zir zir* or a canary-like twitter. It also has a range of other calls which group members use to keep in constant touch with each other.

Due to forest clearance and predation by ship rats and stoats the Whitehead had disappeared from the north of North Island by the 1800s, although it survived on Kapiti and Little Barrier Islands where it remained common. Birds were later successfully translocated to Tawharanui Regional Park, the Waitakere Ranges in the Auckland region, Maungatautari in Waikato, and to many other sites where the species is now common.

The Whitehead is reluctant to fly long distances but can often be seen moving quickly through the canopy. It is an acrobatic feeder and can sometimes be seen hanging upside-down as it feeds on insects and spiders. It will also occasionally take fruit and other plant material.

During the breeding season between October and January it forms very vocal, sedentary groups. The nest is a tightly woven cup, lined with fine material such as moss, and usually positioned in a tree fork or hidden in dense canopy. The birds are very inconspicuous around the nest, which makes it hard to find.

One clutch is laid, usually of three eggs, which is incubated by the female. The male brings food for the female during the 17-day nesting period and then to the young until they fledge at around 19 days. Whiteheads make good older siblings – offspring from the previous year will often help their parents to defend their territory and rear the next year's chicks. They have been known to live for up to 16 years.

This species acts as a host to the brood-parasitic Long-tailed Cuckoo. The Whitehead will incubate the cuckoo's egg along with its own until the cuckoo chick hatches, at which point the baby cuckoo will eject any Whitehead eggs and chicks from the nest so that it can be raised alone by the Whitehead parents.

Whitehead. Shutterstock/Martin Pelanek

Yellowhead

Order:	Passeriformes
Family:	Pachycephalidae
Scientific name:	*Mohoua ochrocephala*
Other names:	mohua, bush canary, houa
New Zealand status:	Endemic
Conservation status:	Recovering
Other information:	The Yellowhead's image appears on the New Zealand $100 bank note.

About the same size of a sparrow, the Yellowhead was the most abundant and conspicuous bird on the South Island in the 1800s. That was until the arrival of rats and stoats. It should not be confused with the non-native Yellowhammer which does not have a vivid plain yellow head, while the Yellowhead will never leave the forest and the Yellowhammer will never enter it.

A predator plague in 2000 drove the last Yellowheads out of Marlborough Sounds and caused the populations to crash in Canterbury, Otago, parts of Southland, and parts of Fiordland where it has disappeared from large relatively unchanged areas of forest. Its last strongholds, with an assessed population of 2,000 birds, are in parts of Canterbury, the Catlins on the Otago coast, and the Landsborough and Dart River Valleys near Queenstown. The population in the Southland hill country of the Catlins seems to be the most stable as the forests there consist largely of red and silver beech where the birds can find plenty of food.

The Yellowhead will commonly forage for invertebrates and their larvae, and spiders, by scratching at loose bark, mosses and ferns on the trunks of trees with one leg hanging onto the trunk and the other leg and tail being used in support. While it's a poor flyer it will easily flit from branch to branch while foraging but will only travel a few metres. It is often located by its machine gun-like chatter before it is seen.

Its nest is a woven, feather-lined cup of fibres built in a tree cavity. This can be anywhere from ground level up to 30m. It is monogamous and the female incubates the eggs by herself over 20 days. The male helps with feeding and caring for the young. The chicks leave the nest after about 20 days, but the parents continue to feed them intensively for several more weeks. Like the Whitehead, this bird is a host to the nest-parasitic Long-tailed Cuckoo.

One of the DOC's conservation goals is to maintain and enhance Yellowhead populations throughout the bird's present range and beyond by halting and reversing the degradation of forest ecosystems.

Yellowhead. © Kathy Reid

Yellow-eyed Penguin

Order:	Sphenisciformes
Family:	Spheniscidae
Scientific name:	*Megadyptes antipodes*
Other names:	Hoiho
New Zealand status:	Endemic
Conservation status:	Nationally endangered
Other information:	2019 Bird of the Year. Its image is on the New Zealand $5 bank note.

This unusual penguin is the only species left in its genus. It is one of the rarest and may be the most ancient of all living penguins. It is certainly the world's least social penguin, contrasting with many other species in the family which breed in noisy teeming colonies. It is known by Maori as Hoiho after its distinctive call.

Previously the Yellow-eyed Penguin was considered conspecific with the extinct New Zealand penguin *Megadyptes waitaha*, which existed 40 million years ago and is known from fossil remains, and appears to have persisted on the New Zealand mainland until about 1500, when it is presumed to have become extinct due to human activity. However, morphometric analysis later demonstrated that the Waitaha Penguin was smaller and genetically distinct.

Up until about 1500 the Yellow-eyed Penguin is thought to have been restricted to the Auckland and Campbell Island groups, while Waitaha Penguin occupied the North and South Islands. With Waitaha Penguin becoming extinct, this allowed straggler Yellow-eyed Penguins to gain a foothold on the South Island. The species was first recorded by Dumont D'Urville, then by George Gray on the *Erebus* and *Terror* Expedition, but it was another 100 years before the first systematic investigation of the bird began.

The average length of a Yellow-eyed Penguin is 65cm and the average weight about 6kg. Both sexes look similar but the male is larger. As with all penguins it is perfectly designed for swimming swiftly through water, athough it also has marvellous agility when hopping over boulders, crossing rough rocky beaches, clambering over fallen trees, or climbing coastal slopes. It requires these skills in order to reach to its solitary hidden nest site, which can be in all sorts of odd places. In general it's a sedentary stay-at-home species that spends most of its time on land rather than in the water.

In 1998 it was estimated that there were 5,000–7,000 Yellow-eyed Penguins, with only about 1,000 left on the mainland. By 2006 there were only 216 breeding pairs

Yellow-eyed Penguin. Shutterstock/Martin Pelanek

on the mainland, where its key breeding grounds are in cool coastal Otago and some coastal areas of Southland where dense vegetation is available including its preferred rimu, miro, kamahi, broadleaf, lancewood, kowhai and ngaio trees. Most of these key sites remain under serious threat from coastal erosion and disturbance by tourists.

Each bird will display strange rituals, gestures and different behaviours, as do people, but the birds obviously communicate with each other. While 18 per cent will divorce and remarry, most form a lifetime bond. When an illicit affair happens, the guilty partner is usually attacked by its outraged mate.

The criteria for nesting sites are shelter, seclusion and a solid back. As a result, nests are well-concealed under dense vegetation so as to be visually isolated from other penguins. Both sexes contribute to site selection. While a pair will return to the same general nest site area each year, they may occupy several nests before laying.

The mating ritual has been described as: 'the sheepish cough, the throb, the shakes, the gawky look, the open yell, the ecstatic flipper beat, the bow, the welcome, the mutual preen, the kiss preen, the half trumpet and the full trumpet.' The typical call has been described as being like the wail of a baby.

Laying usually occurs in September when a clutch of two eggs is laid over a three- to five-day period. Females tend to remain on the nest during the laying period but may leave for a day to feed while the male remains.

Over six seasons, hatching success at the key mainland breeding site on the Otago Peninsula ranged between 81–87 per cent. For the first 40–50 days the chicks are constantly attended by a parent who will wait anxiously on guard duty. They are then left alone at the nest site while the parents feed in the late afternoon or evening, usually coming ashore within one to three hours of each other. Breeding birds will make two feeding trips: a day-trip of 12–20km and a night-trip of less than 7km. On coming ashore, the male or female will often wait for its mate. While they often display affection for their chicks, when irate they will snap at other penguins.

By the age of 20 days the chicks have their secondary down and no longer require brooding. At this point they may wander from the nest site to congregate with chicks from adjacent nests and form small groups until fully fledged after 106 days. During this period individual chicks will begin exploring the area around their nest and go further as their strength and confidence grows. By now a chick will be curious about anything that moves and will peck at it. When it tires it will flop down with its feet stretched out to let the heat escape.

At about six and a half months a chick will weigh about 6–7kg, be as tall as its parents and have obtained its full plumage. At this stage it will waddle out to sea to undertake its first feeding trips, occasionally coming ashore at remote or secluded bays or sandy beaches to rest. Research suggests that only 15 per cent survive to return to their home beach to breed.

Most forage in the mid-shelf region between 2–25km offshore, diving to depths of 120m to obtain bottom-dwelling species such as blue and red cod and arrow squid but they will eat any fish up to 25cm in length.

Potential predators include sharks, fur seals and sea lions, while barracuda can injure them around the feet and abdomen. They are also at risk from plastic debris, fishing nets, oil pollution, overfishing and ocean warming. Human disturbance upsets breeding, and chicks can be predated by feral cats, stoats, ferrets and rats. Mustelids may also take eggs. Adults may be predated by dogs. New Zealand Sea Lions can wipe out a small population.

Heat stress and hypothermia in wet chicks can also be a problem but predation and disease are the major causes of death. Starvation is uncommon but can occur, especially after nine weeks. The main problem is the loss of mature coastal forest. It's thought that this issue alone may be the prime cause of the species' historic decline.

Visitor information panel.

While most scientific work is undertaken or overseen by the DOC, the focus of community conservation groups such as the Yellow-eyed Penguin Trust and private landowners is on active habitat restoration, pest control, and the planting of native vegetation on former grazing land and coastal scrubland. It's also on providing nest boxes in selected sites and protecting nesting birds from human disturbance at unregulated sites.

With 220 birds left in 2020, some regard the Yellow-eyed Penguin as 'The jewel in the crown of New Zealand conservation' and a symbol of hope for the conservation of the country's other threatened birds. Others believe it may be extinct by 2040. This view was reinforced in 2019 when a total of 29 chicks and adults died from avian malaria. This disease, whose vector is the exotic mosquito, was first detected in these penguins in the 1940s but at an incredibly low level. It was found again in the 1990s but still at a low level. By 2019 a change in conditions, including well above annual average temperatures at their breeding sites and well above average rainfall, resulted in many more mosquitos and an associated increase in avian malaria.

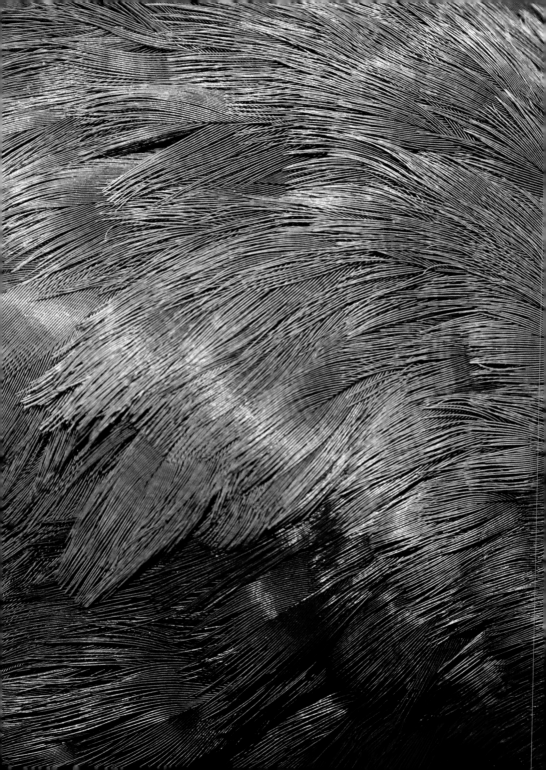

What of their future?

Of the 50 or so surviving species featured in this book, at least 40 are at risk of extinction to varying degrees, so what hope is there for their future? In 2019 a study by Land Care Research, in association with the University of Canterbury and the DOC, found that 26.4 million native birds (used this way the term includes endemics), chicks, and eggs are killed each year in the country's native forests. That's 72,000 birds per day.

As New Zealand's late highly respected conservationist Don Merton put it when speaking of the country's endemics: 'They are our national monuments. They are our Tower of London, our Arc de Triomphe, our pyramids. We don't have this ancient architecture, but we do have birds that have been around for millions of years, if not thousands of millions of years. And once they are gone, they are gone forever.'

Like many other countries New Zealand is feeling the early impacts of global warming. The *Environment Aotearoa 2019* report began with the statement: 'The biodiversity of Aotearoa New Zealand is essential to our culture, identity, and well-being. The whole variety of native plants, animals, microorganisms, and the ecosystems they create is unique to New Zealand and is irreplaceable.' It noted that the country's unique native biodiversity is under significant threat from introduced species, pollution, physical changes to the country's landscapes and coast, harvesting of wild species, and other factors. Almost 4,000 of our native species are currently considered to be at risk of extinction.

Climate concerns

In November 2019 unusually dry conditions in Northland saw forest floors drying to the point where kiwi could no longer successfully prod with their bills while seeking food, and nor could they easily find water. As a consequence, many entered adjacent farmland where the soil had been softened by irrigation to seek food, while some sought water from stock watering ponds or water troughs. Not being able to climb out, they drowned.

Because the country has a comparatively small and confined land mass, its populations of native birds, including endemic species, are more susceptible to extinction than the populations of larger land masses because they are particularly vulnerable to any sudden change. It seems as if once the barriers protecting species in their own communities are broken, the inhabitants are doomed, and island nations are

Takahe plumage. Shutterstock/Spatuletail

at greater risk to this phenomena than larger continents.

Higher evaporation rates and less rainfall means less water in our waterways and more droughts. There will be more intense rainstorms and flooding. The eastern and northern regions will become drier while the western and southern areas will become wetter. Most of these changes will occur in winter and spring. These events will cause mountain snowlines and glaciers to retreat and impact water flows in the South Island.

Any impact on lakes and waterways may also cause changes to stream and river temperatures. This will have adverse effects on the overall health of natural ecosystems and native water-dependent species and will make some waterways more subject to algal blooms. While significant riparian planting has been completed to slow the effects of global warming on farmland, more work is needed. The run-off from dairying and pastoral fertilising operations also needs much tighter control and many farmers are now beginning better to manage fertiliser usage.

On top of all this there will be a greater variation in temperatures and moisture levels, while rising sea levels will lead to higher-than-usual tides. Crucially, the resulting powerful storm surges are predicted to greatly accelerate coastal erosion in low-lying and unstable areas, many of which are crucial to the birds featured in this book, which variously depend upon a significant proportion of the remaining beaches, as well as the coldest forests and a seasonal alpine climate.

If a 1–5°C change in temperature occurs, scientists warn us that the world faces unprecedented climate-related risks and weather events. Whenever there is an increase of 1.4°C in summer, the country's beech and podocarp trees produce bumper crops of flowers and fruit. These monster mast events now occur regularly. What's good for birds also brings an explosion in the populations of rats, stoats and other predators. By late winter and early spring, the seed and fruit have germinated or been eaten. Then the rats and stoats turn their attention to the birds, eggs and young. The country's 2019 mega mast event was the most widespread for 45 years with a projected cost of $20 million required to prevent the endangered species in one key area from becoming locally extinct.

The predicted rate of warming is unprecedented. If, as projected by climate scientists, the temperature rises 1.5–2°C, the effects will be huge. Yet some estimates tell us that the world is heading for a 3–4°C temperature rise. Some believe that even a 2.8°C increase may result in the extinction of between 400–500 of the world's endemic bird species by the year 2100.

Some scientists argue that extinction rates on islands may have always been high and going on for 10,000 years as a random result of genetic effects and population fluctuations before the activities of humans and predators accelerated this process. Some believe that with the assistance of global warming the world is heading for the sixth mass extinction event.

Climate change could also impact on birds in many indirect ways such as effects on their prey, pests and diseases. It may also affect productivity, the number of clutches laid and indeed whether some species choose to breed. Some species will be forced to find more suitable habitat, others may undergo genetic changes to adapt to new situations. As northern parts of the country become drier some migration of trees south by seed dispersing birds may occur, but scientists believe seed and flowering patterns will remain the same.

By 2018, only 29 per cent of New Zealand's native forests remained. While these receive a degree of protection, the outlook is bleak for the country's remaining wetlands which are in private and public ownership and not protected by the International Ramsar Convention or other binding covenants. Since 2001 at least 13 per cent of those on private land have been damaged or destroyed. Despite best efforts. invasive species continue to establish and spread and the demand to convert the remaining wetlands into arable land for farming and to meet urban sprawl is intensifying.

Many studies of late have shown an alarming decline in global insect populations. Over 40 per cent of insect species were found to be threatened with extinction and total insect biomass in many countries was decreasing at a rate of 2 per cent a year. Some scientists believe many insect species could be heading for extinction within the next century or so. Should this happen it is likely there would be no escape for New Zealand where insects are an essential element in the food chain that supports bird life.

The 1080 debate

After many years of trapping and poisoning, rats, mice, rabbits, hares, weasels, stoats, ferrets, feral cats, brushtail possum and hedgehogs continue to threaten the mountain, forest and lowland habitats of many of the species featured in this book. Further, despite the culling and live capture of red deer for venison and velvet farming they continue to damage forest and alpine habitats, as do tahr, wild pigs, feral goats and wallabies. Smaller populations of white-tailed deer, wapiti, sambar, and fallow deer also contribute to the loss.

Despite 60 years of research and practical experience in the design, delivery and use of 1080 poison sodium fluoroacetate (which is a toxic compound found in poisonous plants of Australia, Africa, South America and India) its use remains embroiled in controversy. Some people choose to ignore the scientific evidence proving it is indispensable in controlling possums and many other pests and allowing forests to regenerate. Indeed, in 2019 the New Zealand Society for the prevention of cruelty to animals was forced to acknowledge that it does not understand how it works in the wild and withdrew its call for 1080 to be banned. Some inadvertent by-kill of birds has been recorded in the past during operations using high sowing rates for bait. Even then, monitoring indicated losses were more than made up for by increases in populations after pest numbers were reduced.

Today tighter controls, a significant decrease in the bait-sowing rates and precision applications have resulted in a significant reduction in cost, reduced loss in bird life and with no loss to the effectiveness with regard to the targeted pests. Baits can also be mixed with primary repellents to deter pecking by some species of birds. The average effective sowing rates have also gone down from the 30kg of bait per hectare in the 1950s to less than 2kg per hectare.

Until viable alternatives resulting from research and development are found, it seems that the use of 1080 will remain the only effective tool available for large-scale pest control to protect vast remote and rugged areas from localised bird extinctions. Without its use New Zealand, and the other countries using it, would have unchecked predator populations and ravaged silent forests.

During mega mast events beech seed will be in abundance, every tussock will be dropping seeds, flaxes will have rank-on-rank of flower spikes and other kinds of plant life will be booming. Rodents will gorge on all the seed and their numbers will grow in winter to much higher than usual numbers. Come autumn they will have also eaten a lot of 1080 pellets and every stoat will have a particularly good chance of eating a toxic rodent.

The following four studies indicate 1080 impact on predators and therefore birdlife.

Species	Nesting success prior to 1080 use	Nesting success post 1080 use
Blue duck	3 pairs = 2 ducklings	3 pairs = 6 ducklings
Kiwi	5 per cent survive to 4 years	60 per cent survive to 4 years
Kea	70 per cent success	90 per cent success
Robin	34 per cent success	56 per cent success

In 2019 it was estimated that there were 68,000 kiwi spread across the country. Since 1990, 600 kiwi living in 1080 spray areas have been monitored for adverse effects. None have suffered and there is no record anywhere of a kiwi dying from 1080 poisoning. Without such control nine out of ten kiwi die from predation by stoats or ferrets, assumed predation, or misadventure.

In the past the cost of the final stages of eradication was enormous. When eradicating possums from Kapiti Island, it cost $50,000 to kill the first 11,500 and $220,000 to kill the last 80, and at 10km long and roughly 2km wide it is a relatively small island. Recent advances in related technologies have greatly reduced the cost of such operations. Such technologies are now successfully applied in large land-scale operations over difficult-to-access mountainous and other regions. Poisoning coupled with the use of new generation self-baiting traps is now used to provide the critical cover for smaller forests and remnant blocks on the DOC estate and on council and private land.

Safe havens

Translocations can be financially, logistically and scientifically challenging and could fail for many reasons, among which are chronic stress to the birds during transfer, food sources becoming short, disease and the unexpected arrival of predators. Some species such as Weka and Kea have a propensity to return to their home range, but some notable successes have been achieved. From 1863 to 2012, 148 translocations were undertaken involving 55 species. Of these 41 successfully established new populations. Today five of these species only exist as transferred populations and ten species have increased from a single population through translocation.

It's not just the numbers of a species population that indicates whether it's at risk of becoming extinct. It's also about the genetic diversity within that population. A tiny population with a high genetic diversity may have better long-term prospects of recovery than a larger more homogenous one. When there is slight variation between individuals, there is less resilience in that population to events such as a new disease or parasite or the challenges of global warming. Thus, determining and maintaining genetic diversity within New Zealand's many endangered species, and maintaining a pure genetic line in special cases, has become of increasing concern to conservationists.

Disease pressures

Emerging infectious diseases, defined as 'disease-causing agents that rapidly increase in geographical range, host range, or prevalence,' pose a serious threat to the conservation of global biodiversity.

Avian malaria is one such disease that may affect New Zealand's avifauna. This is caused by protozoan parasites of the genus *Plasmodium* and is vectored by the exotic mosquito *Culex quinquefasciatus*, which was introduced to New Zealand in the 19th century. In recent years it has expanded its range from its introduction sites in Northland and Auckland to as far south as Christchurch.

Blood samples have been taken from native and non-native bird species in selected parks over three summers along with complimentary mosquito sampling. All samples undergo testing that will allow identity to be confirmed through DNA sequencing. For example, initial testing results show the prevalence of avian malaria in non-native species is 10 times higher than in native species.

The New Zealand native mosquito *Culex pervigilans* is suspected of also playing a role in the transmission of confirmed avian malaria in New Zealand. It is hoped that research will provide the empirical evidence necessary for an appropriate management programme to be put in place to manage both versions alongside the other essential management strategies to save New Zealand's endemic and native species – for example, habitat restoration, pest control, captive breeding, translocation, genetic modifications, nest management, artificial insemination and so on.

The DOC monitors the international effects of H5N1 bird flu, although currently the risk of the virus reaching New Zealand is assessed as exceptionally low. It also monitors the country's bird populations as part of its core work and any dead or sick birds found and collected are tested for disease.

Psittacine beak and feather disease (PBFD) is a serious highly contagious viral disease that affects Old World and New World parrots and can persist for a long time in the environment. It is known to be widespread in the North Island where it has spread among exotic parrots such as Sulphur-crested Cockatoo and Eastern Rosella and may have caused some deaths among nestlings. To date it has not been found in Kaka, Kakapo or Kea, but has been detected in the native Red-crowned Parakeet and endemic Yellow-fronted Parakeet, although no deaths have been reported so far. Another pathogen found in New Zealand is 'bird pox' although to date this has had only a minor impact on one domestic species.

Human impact

With increased tourism to New Zealand, the country has improved and is further tightening biosecurity at its sea and air borders to better protect its inhabitants, environment, and economy. The pressure to protect these borders from unwanted diseases, pests and animals has become intense. In 2019 New Zealand received more than 2.5 million inbound shipping containers, with this figure growing annually. Each of these has to be inspected at the border for biosecurity risks, while international travellers are also screened at the border for similar reasons. Despite having stringent import regulations and checks, incidents possessing the potential to threaten New Zealand's avifauna occasionally happen.

Although only partially realised, the projected increase in tourism coupled with natural immigration inflows and population growth cannot help but play an adverse role in the survival prospects of wild species. Outdoor adventure activities are commonly practised worldwide, but the huge volume increase in these activities in the country can only result in increased disturbance at key feeding, roosting and nesting sites for threatened birds.

Damage to key habitats by the unknowing or uncaring is already an issue.

Avian malaria is a threat to the future of species such as Yellow-eyed Penguin.
Shutterstock/Michael Smith ITWP

While New Zealand has laws to prevent these, they are difficult to administer. In the face of the escalating scale and complexity of global travel and trade the New Zealand government is undertaking a full-scale review of the best way forward to create a stronger and more resilient border system.

The pressure to maximise returns from natural resources for the national economic benefit seems unlikely to wane but biosecurity issues are now firmly established in the nation's conscience. Few in New Zealand doubt the need to protect the country's native wildlife and in 2019 the government announced its policy to make New Zealand predator free by 2050 with the focus being on large-scale environmental protection and restoration across the country.

The call to hear the voice of nature is gaining momentum. It is the government's hope that being predator free would preserve the country's threatened species, improve its biodiversity, create greater ecological resilience and restore the country's unique ecosystems. It also believes that New Zealand would become even more admired for its unique wildlife and pristine landscapes.

Many may consider this policy to be aspirational rather than possible. Even if major advances are made to the current tools available, and they can be made available at an acceptable cost, it would still need the support of a high percentage of the urban population to deal with rats and mice and the rural population to deal with possums, mustelids and feral cats across all sections of the country. This is likely to present challenges for the organisers who will have to overcome local, political and in some areas a number of socio-economic barriers.

Despite many holding reservations, the idea of communities being engaged in protecting the country's birds has caught on across the New Zealand with thousands of groups now involved in pest control with the supported of advice and information from DOC rangers and those at local and regional council levels. However, signs are that the take-up is beginning to wane.

The future

Despite some astonishing advances in pest-control technologies and application techniques by New Zealand, a staggering 73 per cent of the country's full endemic bird species, endemic breeders and native birds remain at varying degrees of conservation concern.

The survival of many species seems certain to depend on containment in closely protected ecosanctuaries, but these too will be impacted by global warming and remain at some threat from predators. On top of this there will be the problem of establishing genetic diversity in small populations and maintaining a 'pure' genetic line in key populations. Then there is the particular bias of birds in predator-free enclaves to slow down their reproductive rates, live longer and rear fewer chicks.

Perhaps remnant populations will continue to struggle on in difficult mountain forests and in some other large native forests. Indeed, increasing temperatures have shifted the distribution of some species in the world. However, it seems almost certain that by the turn of the century many of the species featured here will be either extinct in the wild or heading that way, or, along with other New Zealand species, will be found only in museums around the world or surviving in zoos or pest-free wildlife sanctuaries.

Life goes on in ways that are decidedly amazing. Maybe, like many of their ancestors, some of New Zealand's birds will evolve over thousands of years in a changing world into totally new species.

Perhaps, of the hundreds of famous quotes on conservation, this one by Stewart Udall may strike a chord with you: 'Plans to protect air and water, wilderness and wildlife are in fact plans to protect man.'

Appendix A: Endemic Bird Extinctions Following Polynesian Settlement

Most of these species have been identified from subfossils, mounted specimens or study skins taken from both North and South Islands.

Crested Moa	*Pachyornis australis*
Eastern Moa	*Emeus crassus*
Eyles's Harrier	*Circus teauteensis*
Finsch's Duck	*Chenonetta finschi*
Haast's Eagle	*Hieraaetus moorei*
Heavy-footed Moa	*Pachyornis elephantopus*
Hodgen's Water-hen	*Tribonyx hodgenorum*
Little Bush Moa	*Anomalopterix didiformis*
Mantell's Moa	*Pachyornis geranoides*
New Zealand Coot	*Fulica prisca*
New Zealand Raven	*Corvus antipodum*
North Island Adzebill	*Aptornis otidiformis*
North Island Giant Moa	*Dinornis novaezelandiae*
North Island Goose	*Cnemiornis vacilis*
New Zealand Owlet-nightjar	*Aegotheles novaezealandiae*
North Island Takahe	*Porphyrio mantelli*
Scarlett's Duck	*Malacorhynchus scarletti*
South Island Adzebill	*Aptornis defossor*
South Island Giant Moa	*Dinornis robustus*
South Island Goose	*Cnemiornis calcitrans*
Stout-legged Moa	*Euryapteryx curtus*
Upland Moa	*Megalapteryx didinus*

Appendix B: Endemic Bird Extinctions Following European Settlement

Most of these species have been identified from mounted specimens, study skins or fossils that have been collected from both the South and North Islands.

Bush Wren	*Xenicus longipes*
Huia	*Heteralocha acutirostris*
Laughing Owl	*Sceloglaux albifacies*
Lyall's Wren	*Traversia lyalli*
New Zealand Little Bittern	*Ixobrychus novaezelandiae*
New Zealand Quail	*Coturnix novaezelandiae*
North Island Piopio	*Turnagra tanagra*
North Island Snipe	*Coenocorypha barrierensis*
South Island Kokako	*Callaeas cinerea*
South Island Piopio	*Turnagra capensis*

Appendix C: New Zealand's Surviving Endemic Bird Species

Given its truly iconic status the Kakapo has been included in this list, but it can only be seen on either island by arrangement with DOC for special reasons or occasions.

Bellbird	*Anthornis melanura*
Black-billed Gull	*Larus bulleri*
Black-fronted Tern	*Chlidonias albostriatus*
Black Stilt	*Himantopus novaezelandiae*
Blue Duck	*Hymenolaimus malacorhynchos*
Brown Creeper	*Mohoua noveseelandiae*
Brown Teal	*Anas chlorotis*
Fernbird	*Bowdleria punctata*
Fiordland Crested Penguin	*Eudyptes pachyrhynchus*
Great Spotted Kiwi	*Apteryx haastii*

Grey Warbler	*Gerygone igata*
Kaka	*Nestor meridonalis*
Kakapo	*Strigops habroptilus*
Kea	*Nestor notabilis*
Little Spotted Kiwi	*Apteryx owenii*
New Zealand Dabchick	*Poliocephalus rufopectus*
New Zealand Falcon	*Falco novaeseelandiae*
New Zealand Dotterel	*Charadrius aquilonius*
New Zealand Pigeon	*Hemiphaga novaeseelandia*
New Zealand Pipit	*Anthus novaeseelandiae*
New Zealand King Shag	*Leucocarbo carunculatus*
New Zealand Scaup	*Aythya novaeseelandiae*
New Zealand Tomtit	*Petroica macrocephala*
North Island Brown Kiwi	*Apteryx mantelli*
North Island Kokako	*Callaeas wilsoni*
North Island Robin	*Petroica longipes*
North Island Saddleback	*Philesturnus rufuster*
Okarito Brown Kiwi	*Apteryx rowi*
Orange-fronted Parakeet	*Cyanoramphus malherbi*
Paradise Shelduck	*Tadorna variegata*
Rifleman	*Acanthisitta chloris*
Rock Wren	*Xenicus gilviventris*
Shore Plover	*Thinornis novaeseelandiae*
Southern Brown Kiwi	*Apteryx australis*
South Island Saddleback	*Philesturnus carunculatus*
South Island Pied Oystercatcher	*Haematopus finschi*
South Island Robin	*Petroica australis*
South Island Takahe	*Porphyrio hochstetteri*
Spotted Shag	*Phalacrocorax punctatus*
Stitchbird	*Notiomystis cincta*
Tui	*Prosthemadera novaeseelandiae*
Variable Oystercatcher	*Haematopus unicolor*
Weka	*Gallirallus australis*
Whitehead	*Mohoua albicilla*
Wrybill	*Anarhyncus frontalis*
Yellow-crowned Parakeet	*Cyanoramphus auriceps*
Yellow-eyed Penguin	*Megadyptes antipodes*
Yellowhead	*Mohoua ochrocephala*

Bibliography

Aikman, H. and Miskelly, C. (2004). *Birds of the Chatham Islands*. Department of Conservation, New Zealand.

Anderson, A. (1989). *On Evidence for the Survival of Moa in European Fiordland*. Department of Anthropology, University of Otago, Dunedin.

Anderson, A.J. (1982). Habitat preferences of moa in Central Otago, AD 1000–1500, according to palaeobotanical and archaeological evidence. *Journal of the Royal Society of New Zealand* 12(3): 321–336, DOI: 1080/03036758. 1982. 10415351.

Arnold, N. (2018). *Wilderness*, August 2018.

Attenborough, D. (1984). *The Living Planet*. William Collins.

Auckland War Memorial Museum. *Tale of the Giant Moa*. Collections Online.

Baker, A.I. and Daniel, M. (1986). *Collins Guide to Mammals of New Zealand*. William Collins.

Beattie, H. (1953). The Moa: When did it become extinct? First published in *Otago Daily Times*.

Bellamy, D. (1990), *Moa's Ark*. Penguin Books New Zealand.

Beresford, Q. (2012). *Moa: The life and death of New Zealand's legendary bird*. Craig Potton Publishing.

Best, H. and Powlesland, R. (1985). *Kakapo*. John McIndoe.

Birkhead, T.M. (2012). *Bird Sense: What it is like to be a bird*. Bloomsbury.

BirdLife International (2016). *Cyanoramphus auriceps*, The IUCN Red List of Threatened Species.

Birds New Zealand (2014–17). *National Red-billed Gull Survey*.

Birds New Zealand (2019). *Birds New Zealand* magazine 22.

Brown, K.P., Empson, R., Gorman, N. and Moorcroft, G. (2016). *DOC Science Internal Series* 172: North Island kokako (*Callaeas cinerea wilsoni*) translocations and establishment on Kapiti Island, New Zealand.

Chudd, R.W. and Taylor, M. (2016). *Birds: Myth, Lore and Legend*. Bloomsbury.

Braunias, S. (2007). *How to watch birds*. AWA Press.

Buddle, G.A. (1951). *Bird Secrets*. Reed Publishing, Wellington.

Buller, L. (1883). *The History of Birds of New Zealand*. Second Edition.

Bunce, M. and Worthy, T.H. (2009). *The evolutionary history of the extinct ratite moa and New Zealand Neogene paleogeography*. Australian Centre for Ancient DNA, University of Adelaide, South Australia.

Butler, D. (1989). *Quest for the Kakapo*. Heinemann Reed.

Buchanan, J. (2019). *How did our trees evolve to what we have today?* Botanist Victoria, University of Wellington, talk to Kapiti Mana Branch of Forest & Bird.

Canterbury Museum New Zealand (2019). *Fossil remains reveal wren's past*.

Carol, A.K.L. (1963). Food and Habits and Breeding Cycle of the New Zealand Weka. *Notornis* 10(6).

Castro, I. and Morris, R. (2011) *Kiwi: A Natural History*. New Holland Publishers.

Daniel, M. and Baker, A. (1986). *Collins Guide to Mammals of New Zealand*. William Collins.

Davis, L.S. (2009) *Penguins of New Zealand*. New Holland Publishers.

Dieffenbach, E. and Murray, J. (1843). *Travels in New Zealand*.

Digby, A. and Vercoe, D. (2019). Presentation on Saving the Kakapo – the big 2019 breeding season. Robin's Nest, Nga Manu.

Duff, R. (1952). *Pyramid Valley*. 2nd Edition.

Duff, R. (1989). *Notes on Moa Excavations at Pyramid Valley*. Canterbury Museum Records, Vol IV. No.7: 330–338.

Duff, R. The Evaluation of Maori Cultures in New Zealand: Moa Hunters. *New Zealand Science Review* 14: 147–151.

Eason, C., Miller, A., Ogilvie, S. and Fairweather, A. (2011). *An updated review of the toxicology and ecotoxicology of sodium fluoroacetate (1080) in use as a pest control in New Zealand*. Faculty of Agriculture and Life Sciences, Department of Ecology, Lincoln University, New Zealand.

Easton, D.K. and Moorhouse, R.J. (2006). Hand-rearing kakapo (*Strigops habroptilus*), 1997–2005. *Notornis* 3(1): 116–125.

Evans, K. (2019). Return of the lost birds. *New Zealand Geographic* 154.

Fitter, J. and Merton, D. (2011) *Birds of New Zealand.* Harper Collins New Zealand.

Forest & Bird. Bird of the Year website. birdoftheyear.org.nz

Forest & Bird Magazine, issues 346, 350, 351, 352,354,355, 371 and 374.

Froggatt, A. (2019). *Birdwatching For Beginners in New Zealand: A Complete Guide*. New Holland Publishers.

Gault, T. and Hlavacek, P. (2011). In search of the Grey Ghosts. *National Geographic*, pp38–53.

Gibbs, G. (2006). *Ghosts of Gondwana, The History of life in New Zealand*. Craig Potton Publishing.

Gill, B.J. (1999). *New Zealand's Unique Birds*. Raupo Publishing.

Gill, B.J. and Martinson, P. (1991). *New Zealand's Extinct Birds*. Random Century.

Gill, B.J. and Heather, B.D. (1990). *A Flying Start*. Random Century.

Gill, B. (2016) . *The unburnt egg. More stories from a museum curator*. AWA Press.

Goodall, L. (2020). *Maori Conservation Lessons*. Dominion Post.

Hall-Jones, J. (2004). *Fiordland Explored: An Illustrated History.* Craig Printing Co., Invercargill.

Hamel, J. (2001). *The Archaeology of Otago.* New Zealand Department of Conservation.

Hanbury-Tenison, R. (1989) *Fragile Eden.* Century Hutchinson.

Harvie, W. (2019). 50 Million years for birds to recover. *Dominion Post,* 19 August 2019.

Hay, R. (1984). The Kokako, perspectives and prospects. *Forest and Bird,* February 1984.

Heritage New Zealand. *Archaeological Remains of Middens and Rubbish Dumps.*

Holdaway, R.N. (1991). *Systematics and Palaeobiolology of Haast Eagle,* Harpagornis moori*, Haast 1872.* PhD thesis, Christchurch, University of Canterbury.

Hudson, J. (2013). *Call of the Kokako.* The Halcyon Press.

Hutchings, G. (2015). Birds of Prey – New Zealand Falcon. *Te Ara: The Encyclopaedia of New Zealand.*

Hutchinson, J. R. H. (2010) *The Southern Arc. Zoological Discovery in New Zealand 1769–1900.* Century Hutchinson NZ Ltd.

Kapiti Observer, 17 July 2019.

Kapiti Observer, 19 September 2019.

Kelly, D. and Sullivan, J.J. (2009). *Life stories, dispersal, invasions, and global change: progress and prospects in New Zealand ecology, 1989–2029.* School of Biological Sciences, University of Canterbury.

King, M.A. (2003). *Penguin History of New Zealand.* Penguin Books New Zealand.

Kuss, F.R., Grace, A.R. and Vaske, J.J. (1990). *Visitor Impact Management: A Review of Research Work.* National Parks and Countries Recreation, Washington DC.

Lawrie, S. and Powell, J. (2012). *Chatham Islands – First to see the sun.* Deerubbin Press.

Maclean, C. (1999). *Kapiti.* The Whitcombe Press, Wellington.

Manaaki Whenua Landcare Research. *Grey Warbler* (Factsheet).

Manaaki Whenua Landcare Research. *Karaehe,* Issue 26.

Mattern, T. and Ellenberg, U. *The Tawaki Project.* www.tawaki-project.org.

Mattern, T. and Long, R. (2017). Survey of population size estimate of Fiordland Crested Penguin (Tawaki) in Milford Sound, New Zealand. *Notornis* 64: 97–101.

McDowell, R.M. (1969). Extinctions and Endemism in New Zealand birds. *Tuatara* 17(1).

McLintock A.H. (Ed.). (1966). Stitchbird. From: *An Encyclopaedia of New Zealand.*

Ministry for the Environment (2019). *Environmental Aotearoa 2019.*

Miskelly, C.M. (2013). *St Bathans shelduck.* New Zealand Birds online.

Mitchell, K.J., Wood, J.R., Llamas, N., McLachlan, P.A., Olga, K., Schofield, R.P., Worthy, T.H. and Cooper, A. (2016). *Ancient mitochondrial genomes clarify the evolutionary history of New Zealand's enigmatic acanthisittid wrens.*

Moon, G. (2005). *New Zealand Birds in Focus.* Reed Publishing NZ Ltd.

Moon, G. (2008). *A Photographic Guide to Birds of New Zealand* (2nd Edition). New Holland Publishers.

Moon, G. (2009). *New Zealand Wetland Birds and their World*. New Holland Publishers.

Morell, V. (2014). Why Did New Zealand's Moa Go Extinct. *New Science News*.

Morris, R. and Smith, H. (1998). *Saving New Zealand's Endangered Birds*. Random House New Zealand.

Morris, R. and Smith, H. (2019). *Wild South. Saving New Zealand's Endangered Birds*. TVNZ in association with Century Hutchinson NZ.

Nathan, S. (2015). *James Hector: Explorer, Scientist and Leader*. Geoscience Society of New Zealand.

New Scientist, Issue 3217, 16 February 2019.

New Zealand Birds Online. The digital encyclopaedia of New Zealand Birds. www.nzbirdsonline.org.nz.

New Zealand Department of Internal Affairs, Bulletin No.74.

New Zealand Geographic, 8 May 2019.

Norman, G. (2018) *Bird Stories-A History of the Birds of New Zealand*. Potton, and Burton.

Notornis , Journal of Birds New Zealand.

Oliver, W.R.B. (1949). *The Moas of New Zealand and Auckland*. Dominion Museum, Wellington.

Ornithological Society of New Zealand Newsletter, June 2019.

Orbell, G.B. (1986). *The Bird that hid*. In School Journal, Pt 3.

Ormerod, R. (2013). 'Henry, Richard Treacy' Dictionary of the New Zealand Biography. In: *Te Ara – the Encyclopaedia of New Zealand*.

Otago Daily Times, 23 August 1889.

Otago Daily Times, 9 December 2019.

Parker, K.A. (2015). *New Zealand bird translocations, present and future*. Parker Conservation, Translocations, Restoration, Research, Management. Massey University.

Peat, N. (1999). *Kiwi: New Zealand's Remarkable Bird*. Random House New Zealand.

Peat, N. (2006). *Kiwi: The People's Bird*. University of Otago Press.

Pezza, A. (2019). Climate Scientist: Address to Kapiti Mana Branch of Forest & Bird, 27 March 2019.

Philips, W.J. (1963). *The Book of the Huia*. Whitcombe and Tombs, Christchurch.

Poppick, L. (2013). Giant Moa wasn't so giant after all. *Science News*, 19 December 2013.

Potts, T.H. (1870). *Saddleback – Out in the open*. Lyttleton Times, Christchurch.

Proffitt, J., Clarke, L. and Scofield, R.P. (2016). Losing power of flight no impact on penguins' brains. *Journal of Anatomy*. DOI 10/1111/joa.12447.

Radio New Zealand News (2017). *The New Zealand fossil revolution*. 9 November 2017.

Radio New Zealand News (2019). *More than 20 Shore Plover chicks hatch at wildlife centre*. 6 February 2019.

Radio New Zealand News (2019). *Kakapo health continues to decline*. 12 June 2019.

Radio New Zealand News (2019). *World's largest parrot found in Central Otago – and it's twice the size of the Kakapo*. 7 August 2019.

Robertson, H. and Heather, B. (2005) *The Field Guide to Birds of New Zealand*, Penguin Books.

Sage, E. (2018). *Dominion Post*, 10 October 2018.

Scofield, P. and Stephenson, B. (2013). *Birds of New Zealand: A Photographic Guide*. Auckland University Press.

Seddon, P.J., Ellenberg, U. and van Heezik, Y. (2013). Yellow-eyed Penguin *(Megadyptes antipodes)*. In: *Penguins, natural history, and conservation*, pp91–110, Eds: Borboroglu, P.G. and Boersma P.E. University of Washington Press.

Sheeran, G. (2016). *Birds of the West Wind*. CJ Brooks.

Stewart, D. (2018). *The Hunters*. Penguin Random House New Zealand.

Stolzenburg, W. (2011). *Rat Island*. Bloomsbury.

Taranaki Educational Research, Analysis and Information Network (TERRAIN).

Temple, P. (1996) *The Book of the Kea*, Hodder Moa Beckett.

Tennyson, A., Martinson, P. (1956) *Extinct Birds of New Zealand*. Te Papa Press, Wellington, New Zealand.

Tennyson, A.J.D. and Martinson, P. (2006). *Extinct Birds of New Zealand*. Te Papa Press.

Tiritiri Matangi Bulletin 91, ISSN 1171-8595 November 2012

Toki, N. (2018). *Why the survival of NZ's wildlife is in our hands*. Department of Conservation Blog, 22 February 2018.

Troup, C. (2015). Wetland Birds – Grebes and Dabchicks. *Te Ara: The Encyclopaedia of New Zealand*.

Turbott, E.G. (1967). *Birds of New Zealand*. Whitcoulls Publishing.

Vernon, A. and Schneider D. (1991) *The Hoiho, New Zealand's Yellow-eyed Penguin*. Hodder and Stoughton.

Wane, J. (Ed.). (2016). A world-first is unlocking the secrets of our most charismatic parrot. *North & South* magazine, 23 August 2016.

Watola, G. (2011), *The Discovery of New Zealand's Birds* (3rd Edition). Arun Books.

Wilson, K. (2007). Land Birds – Overview. *Te Ara: The Encyclopaedia of New Zealand*.

Wingspan National Bird of Prey Centre, Rotorua.

Winter, M. (2019). Yellowhead. *Wilderness* magazine, January 2019.

Wood, R., Scofield, R., Hamel, J., Lalas, C., Wilmshurst, J.H. (2017). *Bone stable isotopes indicate a high tropic position for New Zealand's extinct South Island Adzebill*. Landcare Research

Wormworh, J., Sekercioglu, C.H. (2011). *Winged Sentinels: Birds and Climate Change*. Cambridge University Press.

INDEX

Published in 2021 by Reed New Holland Publishers
Sydney • Auckland

Level 1, 178 Fox Valley Road, Wahroonga, NSW 2076, Australia
5/39 Woodside Avenue, Northcote, Auckland 0627, New Zealand

newhollandpublishers.com

A record of this book is held at the National Library of Australia.

ISBN 978 1 86966 561 6

Group Managing Director: Fiona Schultz
Publisher and Project Editor: Simon Papps
Designer: Andrew Davies
Production Director: Arlene Gippert

Printed in China

10 9 8 7 6 5 4 3 2 1

Keep up with Reed New Holland
and New Holland Publishers

 ReedNewHolland

@NewHollandPublishers and @ReedNewHolland

Other books by New Holland Publishers include:

A Photographic Guide to Birds of New Zealand. Second edition
Geoff Moon
ISBN 978 1 86966 327 8

Birdwatching for Beginners in New Zealand: A Complete Guide
Alan Froggatt
ISBN 978 1 86966 513 5

A First Book of New Zealand Backyard Bird Songs
Fred van Gessel
ISBN 978 1 92554 641 5

The Lonely Islands: The evolutionary phenomenon that is New Zealand
Terry Thomsen
ISBN 978 1 86966 546 3

For details of these and hundreds of other Natural History titles see newhollandpublishers.com